Iowa Personal Injuries, Car Accidents, Workers' Compensation and Wrongful Death

The Legal Insider's Guide

8 Common Costly Mistakes Made by Injured Iowans *Revealed*
and
Injured Iowans First Fee Schedule™
(Why our Injured Iowans First Fee Schedule™ may be right for you)

Walker, Billingsley & Bair
Iowa Injury Attorneys
Corey J. L. Walker, Erik D. Bair,
Joanie L. Grife & Nicole Merrill

Ankeny 2605 SW White Birch, Ste. 110
Des Moines/Urbandale 7755 Hickman Road
Marshalltown 25 North Center St.
Newton 208 N. 2nd Ave. West

Main Number- 641-792-3595
www.IowaInjured.com

9th Edition

Printed in the United States of America.

ISBN: 978-1-59872-838-5
$19.95

InstantPublisher.com
PO Box 985
Collierville, TN 38027
www.InstantPublisher.com

Table of Contents

Topics	Page Number
Chapter 1- Who Wrote This Book and Why?	7
Chapter 2- 8 Common Costly Mistakes	17
Chapter 3- How Should Medical Bills be Paid?	21
Chapter 4- How You Can Avoid 10 Mistakes in Dealing With Your Medical Providers	23
Chapter 5- Your Time to File a Claim May Be Running Out	29
Chapter 6 Personal Injuries	33
Car Accidents	41
Dog Bites	41
Medical Malpractice/Negligence	42
Motorcycle Accidents	43
Products Liability- Defective Drugs, etc.	44
Semi-Truck Accidents	45
Chapter 7- Damages in Personal Injury Cases	47
Chapter 8- Work Injuries/Workers' Compensation	51
Injured Workers Bill of Rights	55
What is MMI and a FCE?	64
Chapter 411 Work Injuries	67
Chapter 9- Wrongful Death	69
Chapter 10- What Are My Rights as an Employee?	71
Breaks	73
FMLA- Family Medical Leave Act	77
ADA- Americans with Disabilities Act	80

Are You Being "Discriminated Against" The Iowa Civil Rights and Federal Civil Rights Acts 82

COBRA- Continuation of Health Insurance Coverage 88

OSHA- Occupational Safety and Health Administration 99

Do I Have a Right to My Employment File? 100

Employee Drug and Alcohol Testing 101

Chapter 11- What if I Have Been Fired or Quit? Filing for Unemployment 105

Chapter 12- Social Security Disability 113

Chapter 13- Internet and Social Media- Facebook 121

Chapter 14- Do You Really Need an Attorney? 123

Chapter 15- What Do We Do For You? 133

Chapter 16- How Can This Be Happening to Me? Stories of Survival 139

Chapter 17- 14 Myths About Injury Cases 151

Chapter 18- Why Should You Consider Hiring Us? 153

Chapter 19- What Do Our Past Clients Say? 159

Chapter 20- A Sampling of Our Cases, Verdicts and Results 177

Injured Iowans First Fee Schedule™ 183

Fewer Cases Means More Time for Your Case 186

If you or a loved one have recently been injured in a car, motorcycle or truck accident, work injury, dog bite or other personal injury accident you are probably confused or worried about what steps to take next:

- Will I be paid for the time I'm losing from work?
- Will my medical bills be paid?
- What do I do if the other party does not have insurance?
- Will my property damage be paid?
- What if I don't make a full recovery and cannot return to my former work?
- What will the insurance company offer me for my personal injuries?
- How will I know if the insurance company's settlement offer is fair for my injuries?
- How can I find an attorney to represent me who specializes in injury cases?
- How can I <u>avoid</u> hiring an attorney who is <u>not</u> experienced in injury cases?

If you or someone you care about has any of these concerns, then please keep reading this book.

"DISCOVER WHAT INSURANCE COMPANIES DON'T WANT YOU TO KNOW ABOUT YOUR INJURY CLAIM!"

Write any questions, comments or concerns that you may have in the space below:

Page left blank intentionally.

CHAPTER 1

Who Wrote This Book
- and -
"Why Should I Listen?"

Nicole Erik Corey Joanie

First of all, we want to thank you for requesting this book. We have written this book so that Injured Iowans have the inside information they need before hiring an attorney or dealing with the insurance company in the battle for just compensation. As we will discuss later in this book, you do not need to hire an attorney in every case. However, you should have the inside information contained in this book before an insurance adjustor pressures you to settle. We have been featured and recognized by the following:

A Little Bit About Us

At age 14, **Corey** began working for his grandfather Wayne Russell in the concrete construction business during the summer school break. The work was hard, hot, and long, but provided him with framework for his character. His grandfather always told him to get a good education, so he did not have to do hard labor for the rest of his life. Corey graduated from Newton High School in 1990 and played on the 1988 state 4A runner-up football team. After he graduated from high school, his mother purchased an appliance store, and he began working on weekends and during the summer delivering refrigerators, washers, dryers and other heavy equipment. He would also help his grandfather when he needed extra help on job sites. He attended Central College in Pella where he graduated in 1994 and then went on to Drake Law School. After his first year of law school in 1995, he began working at Walker & Billingsley (now known as Walker, Billingsley & Bair).

Erik grew-up on the east side of Des Moines and graduated from East High School in 1993 followed by Iowa State in 1998. While in high school he worked at Hy-Vee and during college he was a laborer with the City of Des Moines in the summer and worked at Mary Greeley Hospital during the school year. He attended Drake Law School where he graduated in 2001.

Joanie is an Iowa transplant as she was born and raised in Virginia where she grew up on the family farm. She worked side by side with her parents' growing apples and peaches and raising cows. She was always active in athletics and received a scholarship to attend Bluefield College in Bluefield, Virginia where she played volleyball and softball during her career. Also, she worked very hard in the classroom completing her Bachelor of Science in Criminal Justice with minors in Psychology and Sociology in only 3 years. She met her husband Rich who grew up in Montezuma while she was attending Bluefield College.

After graduating from Bluefield College in 1997, she moved to Sioux City where her husband played baseball for the Sioux City Explorers. She took a job working as a paralegal, but had her dreams set on law school. In 2000, she started law school at the University of South Dakota and continued to work as a paralegal. She had originally planned to move back to the east coast but fell in love with Iowa. After graduating from law school in 2003, she found a job in Marshalltown. Her husband also found work as the baseball coach at Marshalltown Community College. They have lived in the Marshalltown area since 2003 including living in Haverhill where she served on the city council and as mayor.

Nicole graduated from Southeast Polk High School in 2001 and went onto Drake for undergraduate. She continued her education at Drake Law School graduating in 2008. After law school she practiced at a small firm in Chariton, Iowa, primarily in the areas of juvenile, family, and criminal law, before going to work as an attorney with the Iowa Coalition Against Sexual Assault. As an attorney with IowaCASA Nicole provided pro bono legal representation to sexual assault survivors and their families, with a focus in the areas of family and immigration law. Nicole was hired as a civil rights specialist at the Iowa Civil Rights Commission in 2013. In 2015 Nicole began working as an administrative law judge in the Unemployment Appeals division of Iowa Workforce Development and was promoted to Chief Administrative Law judge in 2019. In 2021, she joined our firm with a wide variety of experience but is now focusing on workers' compensation and personal injury cases. Nicole lives in Ankeny with her two children and many pets. She enjoys travel, being outdoors, and cooking.

Corey, Erik, Joanie and Nicole have experienced firsthand what it is to put in a hard day of work. They have also seen the lives of coworkers changed by injuries. Their years of working hard physical labor allow them to better understand their clients, many of whom have manual labor work backgrounds. They are here to give a helping hand to injured Iowans and help them get back on their feet after a car accident injury.

Together we have been representing individuals against insurance companies and big corporations for more than 75 years. We practice primarily in personal injury and workers' compensation which means more than 95% of our practice involves accidents, personal injury and workers' compensation cases. We worked our way through college and then through law school. With hard work and personal attention we help **Level the Field** Between **Injured Iowans** and Insurance Companies.™

- Experience- Represented More than 1,200 Iowans Injured in Car and Motorcycle Accidents, Work Injuries and Other Personal Injury Accidents
- Active Trial Practice- More Than 450 Trials With 70+ Jury Trials and Significant Appeal Experience
- Corey has www.Avvo.com Attorney Rating of "Superb"- 10 out of 10

- Corey, Erik and Joanie have been named "Top 100 Trial Lawyer" by the National Trial Lawyers
- Corey has been Featured by USA Today, Des Moines Register, Chicago Tribune, KCCI TV, WOI TV, ABC News Radio and Other Media
- Corey Received Award from Iowa DOT for www.QuitDD.com Program Leading the Fight Against Distracted Driving in Iowa
- Corey is a Recognized Lecturer on "Legal Education" for Lawyers
- Practice Primarily in Personal Injury Law including Car Accidents
- Members of the Iowa and American Associations for Justice- Corey has been a Board of Governor for the Iowa Association for Justice since 2001
- Corey was raised in Newton, graduated from Central College in Pella and Drake Law School, has been married to his wife Beth since 1998 and they have 2 adult children (son and daughter)
- Erik was born and raised in Des Moines, graduated from East High School, Iowa State and Drake Law School, has been married to his wife Jessica who is a nurse since 2003 and they have two daughters
- Joanie was born in Virginia but fell in love with Iowa where she has lived since 2000. Her and her husband Rich have 3 children (an older daughter and twins, a boy and a girl)
- Nicole grew-up in Central Iowa and attended college and law school at Drake in Des Moines. She lives in Ankeny now with her two children and many pets.

We realize that your injuries may be the most important event going on in your life right now. Your case will be personally handled by one of our attorneys – not a paralegal.

We represent many people who have been injured by the negligence of others. We have also represented families of deceased loved ones in wrongful death cases. While each case is different, and past results cannot be used to predict future success, we can tell you that we have been privileged to help our clients and their families recover millions of dollars in settlements and verdicts from insurance companies.

Our law firm has 5 attorneys and represents individuals throughout Iowa in car accident, personal injury and workers' compensation matters. To better serve our clients we have fully staffed offices located in Ankeny, Des Moines/Urbandale, Marshalltown, and Newton along with by appointment only locations throughout Iowa, including Cedar Rapids, Waterloo, Davenport, Dubuque, Decorah, Grinnell, Ottumwa, Council Bluffs, and Sioux City. If you are not local to one of our offices, then we can come to you. Also, homebound appointments are available.

Why Did We Write This Free Book?
(Insurance Companies and Lawyers!)

Well, we wrote this book for a number of reasons. First of all, we have heard too many **horror stories** about **insurance companies** taking advantage of people before they have a chance to talk to an attorney. For years one major insurance company encouraged Injured Iowans to not hire an attorney and tried to settle their case early on. Once a case is settled with the insurance company either in writing or on the phone, most likely you will be bound by the terms of the agreement. You may not need an attorney to represent you in your case, but you should be armed with this important information, right from the beginning of your claim.

We wrote this book so that Iowans injured in car accidents have the inside information they need before hiring an attorney or dealing with the insurance company in the battle for just compensation. As we will discuss later in this book, you do not need to hire an attorney in every case. However, you should have the inside information and know the insurance company's tactics which are contained in this book before an insurance adjustor pressures you to settle.

We also wrote this book because our rules of ethics encourage us to educate the public. The preamble to Rule 32 provides:

> As a public citizen, a lawyer should seek improvement of the law, access to the legal system, the administration of justice, and the quality of service rendered by the legal profession. As a member of a learned profession, a lawyer should cultivate knowledge of the law beyond its use for clients, employ that knowledge in reform of the law, and work to strengthen legal education. In addition, a lawyer should further the public's understanding of and confidence in the rule of law and the justice system because legal institutions in a constitutional democracy depend on popular participation and support to maintain their authority.

Frankly, this method of talking to you also saves us time. We have packed a ton of information into this book, and it saves us the hours of time that it would take each day just to talk to all the new potential clients who call. We cannot and will not accept every case and each year we turn down good cases that simply do not meet our case selection criteria. So, rather than cut you short on the phone, writing this book gives us a chance to tell you what you need to know so that you can make an informed decision about what steps to take with your case. Even if we do not accept your case, we would like you to be educated about the process so that you don't become an insurance company victim.

Most attorneys require you to make an appointment in which you would get some of the information that we have provided here. We believe that you should be able to have this information right now, and without any pressure. The hiring of an attorney to represent you is a very important step that should not be taken lightly.

We are also sick and tired of lawyers with a reputation for handling hundreds of cases at a time who have no intention of taking your case to trial, and this book should help you to identify those lawyers before you hire one.

We Are Not Allowed to Give Legal Advice In this Book!

We know the arguments the insurance company will make—and so should you—even before you file your claim. When you were injured, you began a climb up a mountain to regain your respect and financial freedom. The insurance industry spends hundreds of millions of dollars to prejudice the public against you and us. We will be in this fight together. However, we are not allowed to give you legal advice in this book, but we will offer you suggestions and identify potential mistakes. Please do not construe anything in this book as legal advice.

(**WARNING:** THIS BOOK CONTAINS GENERAL STATEMENTS AND IS NOT INTENDED AS LEGAL ADVICE OR LEGAL OPINIONS. THIS BOOK DOES NOT CREATE AN ATTORNEY-CLIENT RELATIONSHIP. DO NOT ACT OR RELY UPON THE INFORMATION IN THIS BOOK WITHOUT SEEKING THE ADVICE OF AN ATTORNEY BECAUSE CHANGES IN THE LAW OCCUR FREQUENTLY AND YOU SHOULD CONSULT WITH AN ATTORNEY WITH RESPECT TO YOUR PARTICULAR CASE. EFFECTIVE FOR WORK INJURIES OCCURRING AFTER JULY 1, 2017, THE IOWA LEGISLATURE LED BY REPUBLICANS MADE CHANGES TO THE LAW RESULTING IN MASSIVE REDUCTIONS IN BENEFITS FOR MANY INJURED WORKERS.)

CHAPTER 2

8 COMMON COSTLY MISTAKES MADE BY INJURED IOWANS

Here is what we consider to be the Secrets to avoid committing one of the 8 Common Mistakes made by Injured Iowans. These are based upon our experience and discussions with many judges, jurors, and attorneys.

1. TELL YOUR DOCTOR "EVERYTHING" THAT HURTS: One of the most critical pieces of evidence is how you feel and how your injuries have affected your ability to function daily. Your doctor is required to keep accurate and detailed records of your medical history and care. The records include your description of how you were injured, your physical complaints, your injuries, the doctor's examination findings, and the treatment you received. The insurance companies will base its offer to you on this critical information. If you fail to tell the doctor everything that hurts, not only will it not be treated properly, but your problems will not be noted in your medical records. If you first begin to complain about some problem weeks or even months after you were hurt, the insurance company will claim that the problem was not from the accident and reduce their settlement offer to you.

2. CONTINUE TO TREAT, GAPS IN TREATMENT: Failing to see a physician regularly is considered evidence that you have fully recovered to the insurance company and eventually, perhaps to a judge or jury. While you should not go to the doctor every day, you need to see your doctors and tell them if you are still having problems. If your doctor says, "follow-up as needed", that means to come back in a few weeks if you are still having problems. If you do not follow-up, then in the eyes of the doctor, insurance company, and jury, you are no longer having problems and have made a full recovery.

3. FOLLOW YOUR DOCTOR'S ORDERS: If your doctor tells you to get therapy three days a week, but you only go once a week, you will damage your claim. The insurance company will say that "you could not have been truly injured, or you would have followed your doctor's recommendations," and will reduce their settlement offer to you.

4. BE CAREFUL WHAT YOU SAY AND DO: The insurance company and their lawyers will use anything and everything they can against you. Even a small lie or exaggeration can hurt your credibility, so the best policy is to always tell the truth. Nowadays, the Internet, Facebook and other social media sites can damage your case. We recommend to our clients that they disable, but do not destroy, all social media sites that they have while their injury matter is pending. We recommend this because if a lawsuit is filed, you will probably be required to provide Facebook and other social media pages to the other side in your case. For example, if pictures are posted of you smiling and having a good time after a personal injury, the defense attorney will show the judge or jury the picture and argue, "Does the Plaintiff look like they are in pain and cannot work"? While the picture may be a short time period where you were living your life, it can damage your credibility and your case.

5. KEEP A DIARY AND WAGE LOSS RECORDS: Few people ever think of writing down how they felt. You need to remember the details of your injury and how you felt on a day-to-day basis. A diary helps to provide accurate accounts of your injuries and how they affected your ability to function daily. Your diary will help you prove the extent of your injuries and can mean a higher evaluation of your claim. Also, it is important that you keep track of the time you missed from work. This includes keeping doctors' excuses for missed work and keeping track of time you miss work for doctors' appointments.

6. DO NOT HIDE PAST ACCIDENTS OR INJURIES FROM YOUR ATTORNEY: It goes without saying that you should be up front and honest with your attorney about any injuries or accidents that occurred before or after this accident. Again, if you saw a doctor or other healthcare provider, then there is a record in existence that the insurance company will find. When you begin a case, the other side will want to know about your prior injuries and how many prior accidents you have been in. While they probably already know the answer or can easily look up the information in one of their insurance databases, they will ask this question to test your credibility. If you have had prior injuries and have been in other accidents, your attorney can investigate this and decide as to whether this is a valid problem or not. Your attorney cannot help you with what he/she does not know but can help deal with this if he/she knows about it. However, if you do not tell your attorney and you misrepresent your medical and accident history, then this can severely damage your case.

7. DO NOT MISREPRESENT YOUR ACTIVITY LEVEL: Insurance companies routinely hire private investigators to conduct videotape surveillance. If you claim that you cannot run, climb, or stoop, and you get caught on videotape doing these things it can be very damaging to your case.

Also, you will often be asked to rate your pain on a scale of 1 to 10. While the pain scale is not usually explained to you, please understand that according to the pain scale, if you had pain at the level 8 to 10 you would be screaming with pain and most likely be in a hospital. Please keep this in mind while answering the pain scale questions.

8. REVIEW AND UNDERSTAND DOCUMENTS BEFORE YOU DECIDE IF YOU WILL SIGN THEM: It is very important that you review any documents sent to you before deciding if you will sign them. We have had clients come to us after they have mistakenly signed a release of their claim. We had to tell them that they agreed to settle their case for a small amount of money and there was nothing that we could do. You should not sign documents you do not understand how they may affect your case but should seek legal advice before signing it. This includes in workers' compensation cases often the insurance company will pay you money consisting of your impairment rating only. The insurance company should pay you your impairment rating **without requiring you to sign** settlement documents. If you have an injury to an unscheduled member (such as an injury to your back, shoulder until July 1, 2017, neck, brain, etc.) then the impairment rating may only be a small portion of what you are owed. Further, even if you do not have a body as a whole injury, you may be entitled to additional benefits from the 2nd injury fund. Sometimes the insurance company will offer additional money for a "closed file" or "compromise settlement". Be wary of a settlement offered by insurance company because it may be far below the fair value of your case claim and will likely eliminate your future medical care and claims for future benefits.

CHAPTER 3

How Should Your Medical Bills be Paid?

In a personal injury case, rarely will the defendant's insurance company make payments for your medical bills. This in true even if their liability is obvious and they have already paid for the property damage, if any. They are not required to make payments and insurance companies routinely make payments only at the time of a final settlement when they can obtain a release. Therefore, you should not count on the other person's insurance carrier making payment for your medical bills until the time of settlement. If your workers' compensation case has been denied or you have a personal injury case, you should look to one of the following means to obtain payment of your medical bills (please keep in mind that I can assist you in choosing the best method to pay medical your expenses):

1. Your own health insurance from your employment benefits package.

2. Your own health insurance that you may have paid for personally.

3. Health insurance obtained by your spouse for your benefit or by your parents if you are under age and living with such parents.

4. For Car, Truck, and Motorcycle Accidents medical payments insurance coverage from your own insurance policy if you were driving your automobile and were involved in an automobile collision.

5. For Car, Truck, and Motorcycle Accidents medical payments insurance coverage from the person you were riding with if you were a passenger in a car or motorcycle that has insurance coverage.

6. www.HealthCare.gov or Medicaid- If you are not covered under an insurance plan you may be eligible for one of the insurance programs under the Affordable Care Act. You should go online, contact a local insurance agent or your local Department of Human Services to find-out.

7. Your own personal funds if you were not insured and are able to pay medical bills as they are incurred.

If there are insufficient funds to pay doctors, hospitals, and other medical bills, our office will help facilitate assignments whereby the client authorizes our office to pay the medical provider directly from any settlement or verdict. These often will serve to satisfy the health provider and often they will wait until the time of settlement rather than pursue collection against you.

Keep in mind that almost all medical insurance policies have a subrogation provision. What this means is simply that they require reimbursement if you obtain money through a lawsuit from a third party. Unless it is a self-funded ERISA plan, we can charge the medical health insurance carrier a 1/3 fee which I pass directly on to you. In other words, if $3,000 worth of medical bills are paid by a health insurance carrier, you would only be required to pay back $2,000. The other $1,000 goes back to you.

CHAPTER 4

How You Can Avoid 10 Costly Mistakes in Dealing With Your Medical Providers?

Whether you decide to hire us as your attorneys or not, I want you to be prepared in dealing with your medical providers after being injured:

1. **Failing to See a Doctor Immediately**

It is your responsibility to prove that you were injured by the accident. If you have any pain or problems, you need to immediately seek medical care. Often insurance companies and juries believe that if you do seek immediate medical attention, then your condition may not be related to the accident. Even relatively minor pain can lead to big problems later so see a doctor as soon as possible, because minor injuries may get worse. The first words out of the insurance company's attorney to the judge or jury should not be, "Mr./Mrs. _________ did not bother seeing a doctor until 3 days after the accident."

2. **Talking With Your Medical Providers About Your Claims**

The job of your medical providers is to focus on your injuries and provide medical treatment. In order to treat you, your medical providers do <u>not</u> have to know about your lawsuit or if you have an attorney. Sometimes they will ask, and you should tell the truth, but your concerns about your case and/or your legal issues should be avoided. Whatever you say in confidence to your medical providers is <u>not</u> confidential when you bring a claim for injuries. Basically, anything and everything you tell your medical providers will end up in your medical records that the insurance company and potentially a judge and/or jury will get to see. However, keep in mind that you will need to tell your medical providers how you were injured. For example, I was injured in a car accident on July 10, 2015 in Des Moines, I was lifting at work and my back went out on August 15, 2015, etc.

3. **Attempting to Hide Your Health History From Your Doctor**

Your doctors and other medical providers will usually ask if you have previously had any injury to the same area of the body which you are having problems. You need to be honest and not try to hide prior problems because they will eventually surface. Your doctors will use your past medical history to diagnose and treat you. If you provide incomplete or inaccurate information, it can not only negatively affect the quality of your care but will likely also hurt your legal case. Eventually, all your prior medical records will be made available to the insurance company. Also, be honest when describing the accident to your medical providers. Do not tell them that your car was "totaled" if the car was repaired. The insurance company and their lawyers will attack your credibility with anything they can find, and you do not want to give them extra ammunition.

4. **Showing up Late or Not Attending Medical Appointments and Therapy**

The insurance company, their lawyers and eventually perhaps even a judge and/or jury will review your medical records. When you fail to attend an appointment, your medical record will say "No show" or "DNS" meaning did not show. While you may have a valid reason for missing your appointment, these still look bad.

More than one "No Show" or "DNS" will not only make your medical providers not happy but may also make it look like you did not care about your medical treatment. Showing up late or worse yet not showing up at all costs your medical providers money because they could have seen another patient which makes then upset. Doctors who are upset with their patients often do not make good witnesses for their patients. If you need to reschedule or cancel an appointment, please call at least 24 hours before it is scheduled. You do not want to hear from the insurance company's lawyer, "Mr./Mrs. __________ missed 3 appointments and for 2 of the ones he/she went to he/she was late. Did he/she really care about his/her injuries?"

5. **Not Informing Your Medical Providers That Your Injuries Are Affecting Your Work**

Your medical records are the heart and lungs of your injury claim and what is in them is very important. If there is no mention in your records of problems doing your job, it is unlikely that the insurance company and/or jurors will not just take your word for it later. Therefore, if your injury is negatively impacting your ability to work, then you need to document this by telling your health care provider. Taking notes with you to your appointments for you to make sure to tell your medical providers everything can be very helpful.

6. **Having Your Pain Improperly Documented in Your Medical Records**

Pain is something that your medical providers cannot feel, see or touch, but are required to document in your records. For the insurance company and a jury to believe that you were in pain, they will want to read about it in your medical records. They will be looking to see how quickly you reported pain after the accident, where the pain was at, how bad it was and how long it lasted. One way to make sure that your pain and limitations makes it into your busy doctor's chart is to write it out beforehand and provide your doctor with a copy of it at your appointment. Your doctors are trained to look for things that are not consistent so please do not exaggerate. If you say that your pain is horrible, but you are sitting comfortably in the office you will likely end up with a negative note in your records.

Pain scale- While you are being treated it is likely that a doctor and/or physical therapist will ask you what your pain is like on a scale of "1" to "10". A "10" is the worst imaginable pain such as being tortured, operated upon without anesthesia, etc.). Few people have suffered pain more than a "8" during their lifetime so please keep this pain scale in mind when being asked questions about it.

7. **Not Taking Medications as Prescribed**

Doctors prescribe a particular type of medication for a particular time period for good reason and you should follow your doctor's recommendations. However, if you think a medication is giving you unwanted side effects you need to call and/or schedule an appointment because your doctor may be able to switch you to another medication. You should not just stop taking the medication on your own because some medications need to be tapered off and also it looks bad when you have to admit that you did not follow your doctor's orders.

8. **Stopping Medical Treatment Too Soon or Not Going For Weeks at A Time**

While no one wants to imagine that their injury is permanent, failing to continue to treat will not make it go away. Juries are people and it seems that everyone is a Monday Morning Quarterback. Therefore, the insurance company and jury will often believe that when a person stops seeking medical treatment that they are healed. They will tell themselves that "if I was still having problems, then I would have gone to the doctor". While this is probably not true it is the way that humans deal with the risk, we all face of sustained permanent injury. Likewise, significant gaps between treatments of say a month or more will be used against you suggesting that you healed from original injury and may have sustained a new one you have not disclosed. If you are still having problems, but your doctor has nothing more to offer so he/she tells you "you are released" or "come back as needed" this means that if your problems do not go away within a few weeks you need to get back to see your doctor. Your doctor may be able to refer you onto a specialist for additional treatment.

9. **Failing to Keep Records**

You need to keep business cards, bills and/or other records of every medical provider that you see. Your attorney will need this information to obtain your records. You should also keep copies of work excuses, restrictions, referrals, and other orders given to you. If you need to take the work excuse to your employer, make sure that you also keep a copy which will help with your case later.

10. **Failing to Follow Recommendations for Treatment of Anxiety and/or Depression**

Pain, limited activities, and disability often cause anxiety and depression following an injury. Conditions like anxiety and depression are just as real as a medical condition that you can see on an x-ray like a broken leg. However, most people cannot overcome these conditions without appropriate medical care and treatment. You can be compensated for psychological conditions caused by your injury so it is important that you tell your doctors if you are having problems and seek appropriate treatment. Unless your mental health issues are properly diagnosed and treated it is unlikely that you will be compensated for them.

CHAPTER 5

How Long Do You Have to Bring Your Claim?

TIME MAY BE RUNNING OUT!!!

Personal Injury (Car, Motorcycle and Truck Accidents, Dog Bites, etc.)

The law imposes rigid time deadlines in which to file suit, provide notice or make claims for different types of actions. These ***time limitation*s** can be as short as **6 months** from the date of the accident in certain types of personal injury cases and never longer than 2 years from the date of the accident (except in some cases involving minors and where notice of the injury is an issue). The failure to act timely to protect yourself can completely eliminate your right to recover! You should consult an attorney to find-out what the time limitation is in your particular case and you should never wait until the last minute to try and resolve you case. In fact, we do not accept cases in which there is less than 3 months before the statute of limitations will expire because there are too many risks associated with waiting that long.

Workers' Compensation

The law imposes rigid time deadlines in which to provide notice and file a petition in your workers' compensation case. These ***time limitation*s** can be as short as **90 days** from the date of the incident to provide notice to your employer. The failure to act timely to protect yourself can completely eliminate your right to recover!

Notice of Injury- Under Iowa Law the injured worker has only 90 days from when he/she knew or should have known that they sustained a work-related injury.

Time to File Claim- Generally, the employee only has 2 years from the date of injury to file a petition with the Iowa Workers' Compensation Commission. However, if the employee has been paid workers' compensation weekly benefits, then the time may be extended up to 3 years from the date of the last payment. However, we always recommend that an attorney review your case well within the 2-year time frame because the risk is too great to take a chance. For example, sometimes an employee has actually not received workers' compensation benefits, but rather has been paid wages, short-term disability or other benefits that do not qualify for the 3-year extension. Note: the payment of medical expenses alone does not qualify. Even though the insurance company may have admitted liability in your case, if your claim is not timely filed you will be barred from making a recovery.

(WARNING: THESE ARE GENERAL STATEMENTS AND NOT INTENDED AS LEGAL ADVICE. THERE ARE MANY EXCEPTIONS AND YOU SHOULD CONSULT AN ATTORNEY CONCERNING YOUR PARTICULAR CLAIM AND THE APPLICABLE STATUTE OF LIMITATIONS AND ANY AVAILABLE EXCEPTIONS SUCH AS IF THE INJURED PERSON IS A MINOR. ALSO, THE FILING OF A CLAIM OR SUIT SOLELY TO COERCE A SETTLEMENT OR TO HARASS ANOTHER COULD BE ILLEGAL AND COULD RENDER THE PERSON SO FILING LIABLE FOR MALICIOUS PROSECUTION OR ABUSE OF PROCESS).

THE WORST THING YOU CAN DO

IS WHAT TOO MANY PEOPLE DO – DELAY OR DO NOTHING!

These days, **<u>doing nothing at all is one of the worst things you can do.</u>** It's hard enough to make ends meet and getting injured should not have to make matters worse. Too many people have told us they wished they had acted sooner before important witnesses moved and could no longer be found, before delays or gaps in their medical treatment proved damaging to their case. We have encountered many people who have suffered serious injuries from work injuries, car accidents and other personal injury cases who failed to seek the "right" legal advice. Some of these people haven't gone to an attorney because they did not know they had the right to compensation; some were intimidated and some had bad experiences with other lawyers in the past.

<u>Note</u>: If you are already represented by an attorney, this book may raise questions for you. We have had countless clients hire us after firing their attorney who did not return phone calls, did not explain the process, were not experienced in handling injury cases, etc. You can still use this book to increase your knowledge, however, we won't take your case if you are currently represented by an attorney!

WHERE DO WE GO FROM HERE?

Write any questions, comments, or concerns that you may have in the space below:

Page left blank intentionally.

CHAPTER 6

What is a Personal Injury Case?

Let's start at the very beginning: Just what is a personal injury case? Lawyers say that they do "personal injury cases" or "accident cases" or "wrongful death cases" and yet what does this mean? A personal injury case is any type of claim where a person has been injured or killed due to someone else's negligence, recklessness or carelessness. These include automobile accidents, motorcycle accidents, truck accident, dog bites, medical negligence, defective products like prescription medications, falls, nursing home injuries and other injury accidents. If the only damage in your case is to property such as your car, then you don't have a personal injury case, but you may have a property damage case. We do not handle property damage only cases, but there are lawyers who do. If you or a loved one sustained an injury requiring medical attention, then you have a personal injury case.

If the negligence, recklessness, or carelessness of another causes the death of a person, then this is called a "wrongful death" claim. The law of each state or jurisdiction differs significantly regarding what can be recovered in a wrongful death case. You need an attorney who understands the specialized wrongful death laws.

What Must be Proven to Win a Personal Injury Case?

The law does not require that a person is compensated for every injury. You must prove that someone else was negligent, reckless, or careless and that because of their behavior you were injured. If you have been injured in an accident that was no one's fault or if you do not sue the right person, company, or business, then the law says that you will not win your case.

You Are At War, But With the Right Battle Plan We Can Win!!

The day you were injured, you entered a war zone. **Insurance companies, special interest groups** and some in the **government** have declared war on injured people and their attorneys. They have waged the war in the media and their propaganda has negatively affected juries. Their efforts to reduce compensation for **Injured Iowans** are called **tort reform.** The success that they have had in tainting the minds of jurors has allowed insurance companies to make unfair settlement offers until you prove to them that you are ready, willing, and able to go to trial.

Common Issues in Personal Injury (Car, Motorcycle and Truck Accidents, Dog Bites, etc.) Cases

What if the Negligent Party has No Insurance?

If you are in a car or motorcycle accident and the other driver does not have insurance, Iowa law requires that every automobile insurance policy sold must include what is called "uninsured motorists' coverage", unless it is waived in writing. If you or a loved one is injured by someone without insurance or injured by a hit-and-run driver then you should review your insurance policy to determine the amount of coverage that you may have. You may be able to successfully sue the other driver, but if they did not have insurance what are the chances that they will have assets that you can collect? Not very good, which is why having sufficient UM coverage is so important. Also, if your case does not involve a car, truck, or motorcycle accident, then the other party may have assets available to recover from or may be "self-insured."

What if the Other Party Does Not Have Enough Insurance?

Iowa's insurance laws regarding cars and motorcycles only require $20,000 per person/$40,000 per accident in insurance coverage. If the responsible party does not have enough insurance to pay for your damages, then you may have a claim under your own "underinsured motorists' coverage." However, under your insurance policy there are requirements which must be met to make a recovery under your insurance policy.

If you were injured, but not in a car, motorcycle or truck accident, then depending on the extent of your injuries the other party may not have enough insurance to pay for your damages but may have assets like property to recover from.

Aggravations- What if I Had a Prior Medical Condition or Injury That is Now Worse Because of the Accident?

Under Iowa Law, you need only prove that an accident aggravated or made worse a prior medical condition such that you sustained further suffering or disability because of it. This means that just because you had a prior medical condition or injury to the same body part, you may still be able to recover damages for your injuries. However, keep in mind that this requires medical testimony from your doctors to prove. This is one reason why it is so important to tell your doctors about any prior injuries that you have sustained.

Previous Infirm Condition What if I Had a Prior Medical Condition That Makes My Injuries More Severe?

Under Iowa Law, if prior to the accident you had a medical condition that made you more susceptible to injury such as diabetes, a prior neck fusion, etc. and the accident causes you to sustain more damages than a person of normal health. Then you are to be compensated for all your damages even though they may be more severe than if your health would have been normal prior to the accident. Also, keep in mind that this requires medical testimony from your doctors to prove.

What if the Insurance Company Asks me to Sign a Release or other Documents?

It is very important that you read and understand all documents that you sign. It is the practice of some insurance companies to send an injured party a settlement and release form along with other documents. If you sign a document agreeing to a settlement, then you have probably signed away your rights. If you are asked to sign documents, make sure that you review them in detail and understand them before you sign them. You may be asked by your health insurance company and/or employer to sign a "reimbursement" agreement for the medical expenses paid. It is important that you understand how this may limit your rights and reduce the net recovery to you.

How Much is My Case Worth?

This is a question we often hear from clients during our initial interview. We tell our clients that every case is different, and we cannot tell you how much your case is worth until we have all the facts. Be careful of attorneys who tell you that your case is worth $XXX,XXX before knowing all the facts to have you sign a fee contract. It is a dangerous practice, unreliable and can cause problems when it is time to try to settle your case. Sometimes doctors will change their opinions, factual witnesses are not able to be found, etc. Once we have gathered all the facts, conducted discovery, spoken with your doctors, and prepared a demand package then we will be able to discuss the value of your case.

Who Will Pay My Lost Wages?

It is rare in an Iowa accident case (not including work injuries) that the insurance company for the other party will pay your lost wages as you incur them. Generally, you will have to rely upon one or more of the following if you are not able to work after an accident:

1. Short term/long term disability insurance you may have through work or purchased on your own.
2. Accident and disability policies you have through work or purchased on your own.
3. Your own personal funds or borrowing money from family or friends until you can pay them back from the money from your case.

Can My Employer Fire Me after an Injury?

This is a question we hear in almost every serious injury case. Unfortunately, the general answer is "Yes". Iowa is an employee-at-will state, and the general rule is that your employer can fire you for any reason or no reason at all. However, there are some federal laws such as the FMLA-Family Medical Leave Act and ADA- Americans with Disabilities Act which provide you with some protection. If you have an employment contract or are a member of a union subject to a collective bargaining agreement, then you may have additional protection such as filing a grievance. If you are terminated after sustaining an injury, then you may have a separate employment law case.
(**WARNING:** THESE ARE GENERAL STATEMENTS AND ARE NOT INTENDED AS LEGAL ADVICE OR LEGAL OPINIONS. IF YOU THINK THAT YOU HAVE AN EMPLOYMENT LAW CLAIM THERE ARE DEADLINES WHICH CAN BE AS SHORT AS ONLY A FEW DAYS TO FILE A GRIEVANCE OR ONLY A FEW MONTHS TO FILE A COMPLAINT WITH THE CIVIL RIGHTS COMMISSION OR EQUAL EMPLOYMENT OPPORTUNITY COMMISSION. IF YOU THINK YOU HAVE AN EMPLOYMENT LAW CASE THEN YOU SHOULD CONSULT WITH AN ATTORNEY RIGHT AWAY.)

Car Accidents

Car accidents are the most common type of personal injury accidents that we see. Just like other personal injury cases, you must prove that the other driver made a mistake also known as negligence or fault. We often refer to this as violating one of the Rules of the Road such as speeding, running a stop sign or red light, failing to yield, failing to maintain control like in a rear-end collision or other violation of the traffic laws. If you are involved in a car accident, the police should be called so that an accident report can be prepared. If the police do not investigate and an accident report is not prepared, it can be much more difficult to prove that the other driver was at fault.

Dog Bites

What do I Have to Prove?

Iowa has "strict liability" for dog bite injuries. Iowa Code § 351.28 provides that the owner of a dog "shall be liable to a injured party for all damages done by the dog…attacking or attempting to bite a person, except when the party damaged is doing an unlawful act" (for example someone breaking into a home is not allowed to recover if he/she is bitten or attacked by a dog). This is a lower standard than other personal injury cases where you must prove negligence, recklessness, etc.

However, even if you were not bitten or attacked by a dog, but for example a dog or other animal like a cow ran in front of your motorcycle or car causing you to be injured, then you may have a claim against the owner of the animal for negligence and be able to recover damages.

Medical Malpractice/Medical Negligence

If you believe that you or a loved one have been the victim of a medical mistake (negligence/malpractice), the first thing to know is that sometimes medical professionals make mistakes just like the rest of us, but many times the injured person will never recover money for the mistake. In fact, our office will not even review a medical negligence/malpractice case unless there has been serious and permanent injury or death. There are attorneys who handle these smaller cases and if your injuries are not serious or permanent you should consult another attorney.

Why only review the most serious cases? Under Iowa law to even get a medical negligence/malpractice case to a jury, other medical professionals (usually other doctors, but in nursing negligence cases it would need to be another nurse) must be hired to testify that there was a breach in the proper standard of care. Also, usually doctors will then have to be hired to testify that because of the negligence the patient sustained injuries. This is what legally is known as proximate cause. As you may imagine, these medical professionals usually charge between $500 and $1,000 per hour to review a case, provide testimony, etc. Therefore, if we are going to advance $40,000 or more in expenses then we want to be sure that there are sufficient damages to make the case worth pursuing.

Something else to keep in mind about these cases is that people (juries) like doctors and nurses. In the last 10 years in Iowa less than 20% of the malpractice cases tried to a jury have resulted in a verdict for the Plaintiff. We tell you this not to scare you away if you think that you may have a case, but so you know that these cases are seldom easy.

Motorcycle Accidents

A motorcycle crash is a violent and dangerous event. Almost 90% of all reported motorcycle crashes result in injury or death to the motorcyclist. The motorcycle itself provides almost no protection to the rider or passenger. Because there are no seatbelts, ejection from a motorcycle is common. If a motorcycle comes to a sudden stop and the rider is ejected from the motorcycle, the rider will likely sustain significant injuries from hitting objects and/or the ground.

Facts About Motorcycle Crashes

1. Approximately 75% of motorcycle crashes involve a collision with another vehicle, which most often is a passenger car.

2. Of the motorcycle accidents involving other vehicles, the majority are caused because the other driver did not detect and recognize motorcycles in traffic. Often the driver of the other vehicle involved in a crash with the motorcycle did not see the motorcycle before the collision or did not see the motorcycle until too late to avoid the collision.

3. Intersections are the most likely place for motorcycle crashes with other vehicles violating the motorcycle's right-of-way and often violating traffic controls.

4. The other 25% of the motorcycle accidents involve single vehicle accidents with the motorcycle colliding with the roadway or some other fixed object.

Product Liability Cases- Defective Drugs, Defective Medical Devices, etc.

The classic example of a products liability case is the Ford Pinto which would explode if struck with enough force from the rear. In the 1970's Ford made a decision to not recall the Pinto and fix it because it was less expensive to pay for the death caused by the product defect. While this is an extreme example of placing money before the lives of people it still happens today in corporate board rooms.

More recently we have seen drug manufacturers bring drugs to the market when they knew there were severe side effects. Sometimes they had conducted drug trials in which they intentionally misrepresented or discounted the adverse effects of the drug. Basically, if you or a loved one have been injured by a product which is either defective in design (for example a drug that has significant undisclosed side effects causing permanent injury) or the product itself broke or otherwise caused injury because it was not properly manufactured, you should consult an attorney to find-out if there is a claim that can be won.

Semi-Truck Accidents

Because of the alarming rise in truck accidents, and because devastation that such accidents can cause people and property, the Federal Government has passed many trucking laws, rules, and regulations that govern the entire trucking industry. However, keep in mind that these are only minimum standards and "industry standards" can require that additional requirements be met. Some of the minimum requirements are:

- Hours of Service- All truck drivers have to take the mandatory rest period between two driving shifts. These rules have been established to alleviate truck driver fatigue, which is one of the leading causes of truck accidents in the U.S.
    - DOT 11-HOUR DRIVING RULE: 395.3 (a.1)-A driver cannot drive more than 11 hours following ten (10) consecutive hours off duty.
    - DOT 14 HOUR RULE: 395.3 (a.2)-A driver cannot drive after being on duty for 14 hours following 10 consecutive hours off duty.
    - DOT 70 HOUR RULE: 395.3 (b.2)-A driver cannot drive after having been on duty more than 70 hours in any period of eight consecutive days.
- Truck drivers are required to possess one trucking license, which is given to them after they have gained the necessary driving expertise and training.

- Trucking companies are required by law to ensure that their trucks are always in top driving condition by carrying out routine truck inspections and following safety guidelines and procedures.
- Truck drivers are required to maintain a driver's log.
- Federal regulations require commercial trucks to carry certain levels of insurance coverage, depending on the nature of the materials hauled. These regulations protect victims of large truck crashes from truck owners who may not have the financial resources to pay damages out-of-pocket.
- Follow both state and/or federal laws regarding driving.

CHAPTER 7

DAMAGES IN PERSONAL INJURY CASES

We want you to know that if you are injured by someone else's fault (also known as negligence) Iowa law entitles you to recover various types of damages:

- **Medical Expenses**: The cost of all reasonable and necessary medical expenses incurred and that are reasonably certain to be incurred in the future because of your injury, are recoverable. These expenses include past (already-incurred) medical expenses and also future medical expenses, which may be caused by the original injury or that result from an increased susceptibility to future injury. All forms of care and treatment, whether hospital, medical, therapy, nursing, diagnostic testing, surgery, physical rehabilitation or pain management are included. You can recover the full value of your medical expenses from the responsible party even if your health insurer has paid all or part of your bills.
- **Lost Wages (Loss of Earnings)**: You are also entitled to recover your lost wages (also known as loss of earnings) caused by your injuries. Wages,

commissions, bonuses and all other earnings and fringe benefits are recoverable. You can recover the full value of your lost wages even if your employer or disability insurance has paid all or part of them.

- **Future Loss of Earnings:** If your injuries permanently limit your ability to earn, you can recover the value of the reduction in earning capacity with reasonable probability which will occur in the future. These damages compensate you for your lost earning power over the remainder of your working years.
- **Pain and Suffering**: This is compensation for loss of quality of life including physical pain and mental anguish you have suffered and will endure in the future because of your injury. These general damages are in addition to and may be far more than the amount of your lost earnings and medical expenses.
- **Loss of Full Mind and Body**: This part of your bodily injury claim is designed to reimburse you for any loss of function or use of your body or mind. These damages are in addition to your other damages described above.

- **Disfigurement:** If the injury causes scarring or other unsightly marks, you are entitled to recover for the disfigurement and humiliation or embarrassment associated with the disfigurement.
- **Damage To The Marital Relationship:** Serious injuries to one spouse may cause damage to the marital relationship. If this occurs, you are entitled to recover for the loss of society, affection, assistance, fellowship and loss or impairment of sexual relations that occurs.
- **Damage To Your Vehicle Or Other Personal Property:** You are entitled to be made whole for any damage to your personal property. When your vehicle can be repaired, you are entitled to recover the reasonable cost of restoring the vehicle to its condition before the collision. In addition, you may recover the cost of substitute transportation necessarily incurred while they are repairing your vehicle. If the cost of repair is more than the value of your vehicle (a "total loss"), you are entitled to recover the full value of your vehicle before it was damaged, plus sales tax.

(**WARNING:** THESE ARE GENERAL STATEMENTS AND NOT INTENDED AS LEGAL ADVICE. CHANGES IN THE LAW CONCERNING DAMAGES OCCUR FREQUENTLY. YOU SHOULD CONSULT WITH AN ATTORNEY WITH RESPECT TO YOUR PARTICULAR CASE.)

Write any questions, comments, or concerns that you may have in the space below:

Page left blank intentionally.

Chapter 8

What is a Workers' Compensation Case?

Let's start at the very beginning: Just what is a workers' compensation case? Attorneys say that they do "work injuries" or "workers' compensation cases" and yet, what does this mean? A workers' compensation case is any type of claim where a person has been injured or killed while on the job. The legal requirement is that the work injury arose out of and in the course of employment. There are 3 basic types of workers' compensation benefits available:

1. Medical Benefits- Lifetime medical benefits for medical treatment, including doctors' appointments, prescriptions and mileage expenses related to your work injury. If your injuries are severe enough, this can include modifications to your home and lost wages incurred by your spouse or loved one caring for you.

2. Healing Period/Temporary Disability (TTD/TPD) Benefits- These are the weekly payments made to an injured worker while they are healing from their work injury and are either not able to return to their job, are only able to work a limited number of hours or are not making as much as they were before the work injury work.

3. Permanent Benefits- At some point the doctors will say that you have healed as much as possible which is also known as maximum medical improvement (MMI). At that point, your benefits change from temporary to permanent. If your condition heals and you are left with no permanent problems, then you probably do not have a claim for permanent disability benefits. If you have a

permanent impairment rating and/or permanent restrictions, then you are likely owed permanent disability benefits.

What Must be Proven to Win a Work Injury Case?

The law does not require that a person is compensated for every work injury. You must prove that you were on the job working when you were injured. However, please keep in mind that there are special exceptions like falling in the employer's parking lot which are also considered a work injury, horseplay which is not considered a work injury, etc.

What if I Previously Sustained an Injury and I am Injured Again? Aggravations

Under Iowa law, you need only prove that a work injury caused a material and substantial aggravation of a preexisting condition for it to be considered a work injury. That means just because you have had a prior injury to the same body part, you may still be entitled to benefits.

Also, if you previously sustained a scheduled member injury (arm, leg, etc.), whether or not it was work related, and then you sustain another scheduled member injury then you may be entitled to additional benefits under the Iowa Second Injury Fund. If you qualify for 2nd Injury Fund benefits then the extent of your permanent disability benefits will be based upon the factors used when determining industrial disability just like a back, neck or brain injury. (Note: for shoulder injuries which occur after July 1, 2017, the law has been changed. These changes are explained in more detail on p. 59 of this book).

What if I Was Hurt in Iowa, but My Company is From Another State?

Generally, the Iowa Workers' compensation system has jurisdiction over all injuries which occur within the state of Iowa subject to a few exceptions. Iowa Code § 85.3 and 85.72.

What if I Was Hurt Outside The State of Iowa?

Depending on the language of your employment contract, where you were hired, time spent in Iowa or other factors, you may still have an Iowa Workers' compensation claim. For example, it is common for Iowa trucking companies to put language in their contracts that if you are hurt at work, you agree that you will have an Iowa Workers' compensation claim. It is not necessarily a bad thing to have an Iowa case because compared to other states, Iowa has some of the best benefits available.

Can I Sue My Employer For Pain and Suffering?

No, generally you are not allowed to sue your employer for pain and suffering. When the Iowa Workers' Compensation statute was passed in 1913, there was a trade-off made between employers and employees. While an employee does not have to prove fault or negligence like they would in a car accident case for instance, the trade-off is that the employee is not allowed to recover pain and suffering damages. Under what is known as the "exclusive remedy doctrine", an employee generally only has a workers' compensation claim against his or her employer for work injuries. There are exceptions to this rule such as what is known as "gross negligence" and you should consult an attorney to find-out if your case meets one of the exceptions.

You need an attorney who understands the specialized workers' compensation laws.

THE INJURED WORKERS' BILL OF RIGHTS

Iowa Law has recognized the needs of its injured workers since 1913. The law requires every employer to obtain workers' compensation insurance (or for the employer to register with the State of Iowa as being self-insured) to cover their workers. Even the best employer, however, is not likely to tell you all you need to know. If you are injured in a work accident or suffer from an occupational disease caused by your work, then Iowa law says that you have the following rights:

(**WARNING:** THESE ARE GENERAL STATEMENTS AND NOT INTENDED AS LEGAL ADVICE. CHANGES IN THE LAW OCCUR FREQUENTLY. YOU SHOULD CONSULT WITH AN ATTORNEY CONCERNING YOUR PARTICULAR CASE.)

1. Lifelong Medical Care: Your employer and/or their insurance company are responsible for paying for all medical care necessary to treat your work-related injury. This includes all forms of care and treatment, whether hospital, medical, therapy, nursing, diagnostic testing, surgery, physical rehabilitation, or pain management. However, generally your employer and/or their insurance company get to choose your medical providers. The right to medical care and treatment may continue for the rest of your life for conditions related to your work injury or occupational disease.

2. Right to Medical Treatment: You always have the right to seek medical care from any medical provider that you choose. However, please keep in mind that your employer and/or their insurance carrier will generally only pay for medical care that they have authorized or approved.

Also, if you have health insurance, they may reject the claim as being a work-related condition.

3. Payment of Medical Care Including Mileage:

- **Medical Expenses:** Generally, your employer and/or their insurance company has to provide you with medical care and treatment. This includes them paying for all treatment that they offer to you. If your injuries are severe enough, this can include modifications to your home and lost wages incurred by your spouse or loved one caring for you. Also, there are circumstances when they can be held responsible for paying medical expenses that you incur with medical providers not approved by them. For example, if your work injury claim has been denied, they lose control over your medical treatment and may be responsible for paying the bills. There are other limited circumstances when you can seek medical care with a provider who is not approved, and they will be required to pay for it.

- **Mileage Expenses:** You are entitled to be reimbursed at the following rates for all mileage you incur going to and from doctors' appointments, physical therapy visits, etc. for travel during the time periods listed:

    $.535 per mile- July 1, 2017, to June 30, 2018
    $.545 per mile- July 1, 2018, to June 30, 2019
    $.58 per mile- July 1, 2019, to June 30, 2020
    $.575 per mile- July 1, 2020, to June 30, 2021
    $.56 per mile- July 1, 2021, to June 30, 2022

(Note: the mileage amount usually changes every July 1)

4. **Right to Refuse Medical Care:** You have the right to refuse any medical procedures or care that you do not want. For example, if the company doctor recommends surgery, you do not have to proceed with surgery. However, please keep in mind that not proceeding with surgery may have an impact upon your case.

5. **Weekly Check While You Recover And Cannot Work:** While you are healing and unable to work, you will receive weekly checks to replace your usual earnings. This applies both if you are completely unable to work (known as TTD- temporary total disability benefits) or if you return to work but are working less than 40 hours per week (known as TPD- temporary partial disability benefits). The amount of your weekly payment is called your "rate" which is discussed below.

Rate: The amount of your weekly payments, also known as your "weekly benefits", is based upon your average earnings prior to the work injury, known as your AWW- Average Weekly Wage. If you are paid on an hourly basis, generally your rate will be based upon your average wages for a 13-week period prior to your work injury, excluding short weeks (weeks in which you should have, but did not work a full 40 hours for a reason like illness, etc). Your weekly rate is based upon your marital status, your number of exemptions, and your AWW- Average Weekly Wage multiplied times 80% of your spendable weekly earnings. For a link to the chart where you can look-up your rate based upon AWW, etc. go to www.IowaWorkInjuryRate.com.

There is no minimum rate for TTD- Temporary Total Disability benefits or TPD- Temporary Total Disability benefits. TTD benefits are paid at your weekly rate while TPD is calculated based upon the amount of your

AWW: Average Weekly Wages minus what you are making while working either a different job for less money or less hours X 2/3. For example, if you were making $600 per week before you were injured and the doctor has released you to work 4 hours per day at your normal hourly rate of $15 per hour then you would be making $300 per week. $600 - $300 = $300 X 2/3 = $200 in TPD benefits in addition to the wages you make while working 4 hours per day.

PPD: There is both a minimum and a maximum average weekly wage for permanent disability benefits based upon the statewide average weekly wage. These amounts change each year and for work injuries which occurred from July 1, 2021, to until June 30, 2022, the minimum- AWW- Average Weekly Wage is $351 and the maximum is $1,845. If your work injury occurred before or after this time frame you can find a link to the amounts at www.IowaWorkInjuryRate.com.

Your rate is very important because it determines how much compensation you receive. For example, if you are owed 100 weeks of benefits and your rate is $252 then your total compensation is $25,200 paid weekly. However, if you are owed 100 weeks of benefits and your rate is $575 your total compensation is $57,500 paid weekly. Our experience is that in about **50% of our cases**, the employer/insurance company has **underpaid the employee** by using a lower weekly rate **than what is owed**. That is why in every case we verify that you have been paid the proper rate as it can make thousands of dollars of difference.

6. Money for Permanent Disability: If your work injury or occupational disease causes a permanent disability also known as a permanent impairment rating or functional impairment rating, then you are entitled to money for the resulting disability. The amount of the benefits is based upon the body part(s) involved, the nature and extent of your disability and the amount of your average weekly earnings prior to your work injury.

Examples of Unscheduled Member Injuries:

Shoulder- Percentage based upon 500 weeks of available benefits. For example, an 8% body as a whole shoulder impairment rating generally equals a minimum of 40 weeks of benefits. However, depending on many factors, including lifting and activity restrictions imposed, lost wages, etc. an 8% shoulder impairment rating could result in 100 weeks or more in benefits. (Note: for shoulder injuries occurring after July 1, 2017, because of legislation passed by Republicans, some shoulder injuries may be considered scheduled member injuries and compensation is only based upon a percentage of 400 weeks which has not yet been defined. Keep in mind that if you had a distal clavicle excision, problems with your neck, injuries to your labrum, etc. then you may still qualify as an unscheduled injury. You should consult with a qualified work injury attorney for more information).

Back- Percentage based upon 500 weeks of available benefits. For example, a 10% body as a whole back impairment rating generally equals a minimum of 50 weeks of benefits. However, depending on many factors including lifting and activity restrictions imposed, lost wages, etc. a 10%

back impairment rating could result in 120 weeks or more in benefits.

Neck- Percentage based upon 500 weeks of available benefits. For example, a 15% body as a whole neck impairment rating generally equals a minimum of 75 weeks of benefits. However, depending on many factors including lifting and activity restrictions imposed, lost wages, etc. a 15% neck impairment rating could result in 150 weeks or more in benefits.

Brain and Mental Injuries- Percentage based upon 500 weeks of available benefits. Sometimes you will not receive an impairment rating for a brain injury or mental health injuries such as depression, anxiety or PTSD- post traumatic stress disorder. However, if you have a permanent brain or mental health condition which has impacted your ability to earn a living then you may be entitled to receive permanent disability benefits.

Burns to Skin and Nerve Injuries- CRPS/RSD (Chronic Regional Pain Syndrome)- Even if your work injury is to a scheduled member, if you have sustained a burn or been diagnosed with one of the above nerve injuries or another type of nerve injury then your case may be considered an injury to your body as a whole. Depending on many factors including your ability to work, lifting and activity restrictions imposed, lost wages, etc. you may be entitled to a percentage of 500 weeks of benefits.

Respiratory and Circulation Injuries- These injuries include occupational asthma and injuries to arms or other body parts when the circulation has been affected like in Reynaud's syndrome.

Examples of Scheduled Member Injuries:

Arm- 250 weeks, e.g. a 10% arm impairment rating equals 25 weeks of benefits.

Hand- 190 weeks, e.g. a 20% hand impairment rating equals 38 weeks of benefits.

Leg- 220 weeks, e.g. a 15% leg impairment rating equals 33 weeks of benefits.

Foot- 150 weeks, e.g. a 30% foot impairment rating equals 45 weeks of benefits.

Fingers- Thumb- 60 weeks, 1st Finger- 35 weeks, 2nd Finger- 30 weeks, 3rd Finger- 25 weeks, 4th Finger- 20 weeks. For example, a 40% impairment rating to the 1st finger would equal 14 weeks of benefits. Please note that injuries to fingers may not count as an injury to a hand for 2nd injury fund or other purposes.

NOTE: If you do not know which category your injury fits into, please contact us. Also, you may be entitled to additional benefits for a scheduled member injury depending on whether or not you have sustained previous injuries, etc. For example, you may qualify for 2nd Injury Fund benefits.

- 2nd Injury Fund: If you previously sustained a scheduled member injury (arm, hand, leg, knee, foot, eye, etc.) even if it was not work related, and then sustain a work-related scheduled member injury you may be entitled to additional benefits under the Iowa Second Injury Fund Act. Please keep in mind that prior medical conditions such as arthritis, carpel tunnel, vision loss, etc. followed by a scheduled member work related injury may qualify you for additional benefits. If you think that you may qualify for the 2nd injury fund, please give us a call and we can help you determine if you qualify.

- Permanent Total Disability: If you sustain an unscheduled member injury, injuries to both hands, arms or legs; or a qualifying 2nd Injury and are no longer able to do any work, then you may be entitled to receive permanent total disability benefits which pay you a weekly benefit for the rest of your life.

- Death: Damages for the death of a worker are available for the wife, husband, and/or dependent children of the deceased. This can include a spouse if there was a common law marriage. Also, sometimes people who were not related, but dependent upon the deceased may recover. Damages are compensation for the lifetime of the beneficiary.

- Additional Disability Benefits If Your Condition Worsens: You may be able to "re-open" your claim after an initial disability award if the injury worsens. The request to "re-open" your claim MUST BE MADE WITHIN THREE YEARS of the date on which you last received workers' compensation disability benefits.

7. Independent Medical Examination: Once the doctors have said that you will not make further improvement, you have reached MMI, you have the right to have an independent medical examination performed by a doctor of your own choosing for an impairment rating and permanent restrictions. There are several doctors that I will recommend depending on the nature of your injury.

8. Right to Your Job- Under Iowa law your employer is not supposed to fire you for filing a workers' compensation claim. However, you can be terminated for other reasons such as absences, work problems, etc. Also, subject to some exceptions (for example if you are a union member) generally your employer does not have to find you work if you are unable to return to your old job because of restrictions.

9. Right to Find Another Job- Leaving your job does not end your workers' compensation claim. Just because you may be receiving workers' compensation benefits, does not mean that you have to remain employed with the same employer. However, leaving your job while you are still being treated may impact your case and the compensation that you receive.

10. Right to Seek Alternative Medical Care- If the medical care offered by your employer and/or their insurance company is not reasonable then you may file a petition for alternative medical care. However, please keep in mind that there are specific legal requirements that must be completed before filing such a petition. Also, if the employer denies liability in your case then the petition will be dismissed.

What Does MMI Mean and Why are They Ordering a FCE?

A FCE is usually ordered once you have reached maximum medical improvement referred to as MMI. Once you are at MMI, in the opinion of the doctor you are treating with, you are as good as you are going to get. Do not let this discourage you because there are many doctors with many different opinions. You are always allowed to seek medical

care and treatment on your own, but usually it will be at your own expense, unless you are successful in obtaining alternative medical care described elsewhere in this book. Also, keep in mind that you have the right to a 2nd opinion once their doctor says you are at MMI and has evaluated you for a permanent impairment rating. Your right to a 2nd opinion is discussed in more detail elsewhere in this book.

What is an FCE- Functional Capacity Evaluation or Examination?

A Functional Capacity Evaluation (called FCE for short) is testing done by a physical therapist. It usually involves a series of physical tests performed at the request of the physical therapist. The process can take from a few hours to more than 6 hours over 2 days. The length of the FCE will depend upon who the physical therapist is and what type of FCE they will be performing. There are several different FCE systems which are designed to determine what you should and should not do given your physical issues.

What Can I Expect at the FCE?

First of all, please keep in mind that under Iowa law you are not required to attend a FCE examination but failing to attend one can have a significant impact on your case. If you are not comfortable with proceeding with a FCE you should contact a qualified work injury attorney to discuss the specifics in your case so you can decide what is best for you. Also, there are many very important things you should know about what to do and not to do during the evaluation. Here are some of the tips we provide to our clients when attending a FCE:

1. Giving Your Best, "Full Effort"- You should try hard and give a full and honest effort in the tests without injuring yourself. There are a number of tests built into the evaluation that will determine if you are giving full effort. Therefore, even if the therapist tests an area of your body that was not injured, you still need to give full effort. One of the keys to the FCE test is that as long as someone comes in and gives their very best effort during the test, then it should result in a valid test.

2. Restrictions- if you are currently under restrictions given by one or more doctors I would recommend that you bring your written restrictions with you to the FCE and show the therapist these prior to the evaluation.

3. Medications- I would recommend that you do not take your pain medications in the morning on the day of the examination, unless you know that your employer will allow you to take the pain medications while working.

4. The therapist is not your friend, and you need to be careful about what you say. It is not the time to make "wise-cracks"; say negative things about the insurance company, your employer, the defense attorney, your doctors, or anyone else for that matter; or exaggerate your symptoms. For example, if you tell the therapist that you can only sit for 5 minutes at a time, then you better be standing up every 5 minutes or they will record this as being inconsistent with what you said. The therapist will write down in his/her report what you tell them so be honest and stay with the facts.

5. You need to make sure that you fully understand the therapist's instructions as to when you should stop an activity before performing the test. For example, if the therapist tells you to continue the exercise until the pain increases to the point where it is uncomfortable, ask the therapist to define that for you. Does it mean that you would be uncomfortable doing it every day at work or that it causes you increased pain? Make sure that you understand when the therapist wants you to stop.

A FCE is a very important part of your workers' compensation case and can significantly impact if you are able to go back to your job, how much compensation you receive, etc. The above represents just some of the tips we provide to our clients along with a detailed consultation, so they are fully prepared and know what to expect at the FCE.

What is a Chapter 411 Injury Claim?

If you are a police officer or fire fighter who works for a larger city (for example, Ames, Ankeny, Bettendorf, Boone, Des Moines, . . .) then chances are that your claim will not be handled under the Iowa Workers' compensation system described previously, but rather under Chapter 411 of the Iowa Code. At last count there were 49 cities who participate in the Chapter 411 system instead of the workers' compensation system. A few of the cities cover only the police under Chapter 411 while fire personnel are covered under workers' compensation. If you wonder which system you are covered under feel free to give us a call and we can look at the most recent list of cities.

There are many differences between the Chapter 411 system and the workers' compensation system including that Chapter 411 is a retirement system and provides compensation for both work injuries and non-work-related injuries. Also, under Chapter 411, compensation can increase for injuries based upon the number of years you have worked for a city covered under the system.

In order to qualify for permanent disability benefits you must:

1. Be off work for sixty or more days due to the disability;

2. If the city expects your injuries to be permanent then they are to notify the Chapter 411 compensation system;

3. Have a medical examination by a provider chosen by the medical board; and

4. Have a hearing before the medical board and if the board certifies that you are "mentally or physically incapacitated for further performance of duty and that the incapacity is likely to be permanent, and that the member should be retired" then you will receive disability benefits.

Note: There are many very specific requirements concerning the amount of benefits that you receive under Chapter 411, but here are a few examples:

For "accidental disability" (meaning work related) then you shall receive 60% of your average final compensation or the retirement allowance that you would have received if you had attained 55 years of age.

For "ordinary disability" (meaning not work related) if you have 5 or more years of membership service the amount you are paid is 50% of your average final compensation if you had attained 55 years of age. If you have less than 5 years of membership then the amount is 25% of the average final compensation.

Chapter 9

Wrongful Death

If the negligence, recklessness or carelessness of another causes the death of a person, then this is called a "wrongful death" claim. The law of each state or jurisdiction differs significantly regarding what can be recovered in a wrongful death case. Proving liability for a wrongful death personal injury claim is the same as any other personal injury case. However, the damages for "wrongful death" are different. Generally, the dependents (usually the wife, husband, parent or child) may be entitled to damages. Damages are not limited to economic loss and may include damages for loss of consortium which the law defines as loss of companionship, comfort, guidance, affection and aid the relationship, general usefulness, industry and attention within the home and family. Damages are also available for the deceased's lost accumulation of value to his/her Estate, pre-death pain and suffering and interest on burial expenses.

Workers' Compensation- Damages for the death of a worker are available for the wife, husband, and/or dependent children of the deceased. This can include a spouse if there was a common law marriage. Also, sometimes people who were not related, but dependent upon the deceased may recover. Damages are compensation for the lifetime of the beneficiary and also include burial expenses not to exceed 12 times the statewide average weekly wage in effect at the time of death in addition to the weekly death benefits.

Write any questions, comments, or concerns that you may have in the space below:

Page left blank intentionally.

CHAPTER 10

What Are My Rights As An Employee?

This is a question we hear almost everyday when talking to people. First of all, Iowa is an employee-at-will state and the general rule is that your employer can fire you or demote you for any reason or no reason at all. However, if you have an employment contract or are a member of a union subject to a collective bargaining agreement then you may have additional protection and may be able to file a grievance and keep your job. Also, there are some federal laws such as FMLA- Family Medical Leave Act and ADA- Americans with Disabilities Act which provide you with some protection. Finally, if you can prove that you were fired because you filed a workers' compensation claim or because of your age, sex, race, religion, etc. then you may have a separate employment law case for a violation of the Iowa or Federal Civil Rights Act. Your specific rights are explained in more detail in the chapters devoted to each subject.

(**WARNING:** THESE ARE GENERAL STATEMENTS AND ARE NOT INTENDED AS LEGAL ADVICE OR LEGAL OPINIONS. IF YOU THINK THAT YOU HAVE AN EMPLOYMENT LAW CLAIM THERE ARE DEADLINES WHICH CAN BE AS SHORT AS ONLY A FEW DAYS TO FILE A GRIEVANCE OR ONLY A FEW MONTHS TO FILE A COMPLAINT WITH THE CIVIL RIGHTS COMMISSION OR EQUAL EMPLOYMENT OPPORTUNITY COMMISSION. IF YOU THINK YOU HAVE AN EMPLOYMENT LAW CASE THEN YOU SHOULD CONSULT WITH AN ATTORNEY RIGHT AWAY.)

<u>Real Life Examples</u>: We know that you just want to go to get better and enjoy a good life away from work. There are many laws that can protect you and your job that you should at least have some familiarity with. Here are some real-life examples of employees who made costly mistakes.

A RN who worked at a Des Moines hospital fell on ice at home and badly broke her ankle. Thankfully, she qualified for the FMLA and was able to take time off to heal. She was not automatically paid just because she had FMLA pay, but thankfully had enough accrued sick time and qualified for short-term disability benefits so she was able to pay her bills. She returned to work after 10 weeks, but in the meantime became pregnant. Because of the timing of her leave, once she had her baby, she only had 2 weeks of FMLA leave time left, but decided to take 12 weeks of maternity leave. Her employer would not agree to more than 2 weeks of leave, and she ended up losing her job with the hospital as she was terminated for missing too much time from work. Yes, the FMLA can provide you with protection, but it is not unlimited.

A client of ours injured his back while doing some heavy lifting in the factory where he worked. He was sent to the company doctor and immediately taken off work. Unfortunately, his back did not improve, and an MRI revealed that he had two herniated discs in is back, L4-5 and L5-S1. The doctor recommended a lumbar fusion surgery which he had. His employer was not willing or able to bring him back on light duty/restricted duty and he missed several months of work. In the meantime, his employer decided they needed someone to fill his job, so they hired someone else. Because he had used up his 12 weeks of FMLA time, even though it was a work injury his employer was allowed to fire him. He made the mistake of not contacting our office until the insurance company had stopped his weekly checks, but once he met with us, we were able to get his weekly benefits started again and get him unemployment. He also had a potential ADA case that we investigated.

Do I Have a Right to Breaks at Work?

There are no laws in Iowa that require your employer to give you breaks if you are 18 or older, subject to federal laws concerning breast feeding set-forth below. Also, even if your employer does give you breaks, they do not have to pay you while you are on break. Further, your employer can require you to stay at their business during your break. There are a few exceptions to the break rule including the following:

1. All employees must be allowed toilet breaks when needed.
2. Workers covered by union contract who don't receive contract- promised breaks should contact their union representative.
3. Minors younger than 16 must be given a 30-minute break if they are employed five hours or more in a day.
4. Certain other limited categories of workers, such as airline pilots, may be entitled to mandatory breaks under applicable regulations. Check with the appropriate regulatory agency for such regulations.

Breast Feeding- Employers are required to provide a "reasonable break time for an employee to express breast milk for her nursing child for 1 year after the child's birth each time such employee has need to express the milk." Employers are also required to provide "a place, other than a bathroom, that is shielded from view and free from intrusion from coworkers and the public, which may be used by an employee to express breast milk."

A bathroom, even if private, is not a permissible location under the Act. The location provided must be functional as a space for expressing breast milk. If the space is not dedicated to the nursing mother's use, it must be available when needed in order to meet the statutory requirement. A space temporarily created or converted into a space for expressing milk or made available when needed by the nursing mother is sufficient provided that the space is shielded from view, and free from any intrusion from co-workers and the public.

(Note: An employer is not required to pay the employee for breast feeding breaks. Also, an employer that employs less than 50 employees shall not be subject to these requirements, if they would impose an undue hardship causing the employer significant difficulty or expense when considered in relation to the size, financial resources, nature or structure of the employer's business.)

Is There a Limit on the Number of Hours That I am Required to Work?

For most employees there is no limit of the number of hours unless there is an employment agreement or contract that says otherwise. Many employers give rest and meal breaks due to health and safety concerns. There are limits on the number of hours children under age 16 can work, and some contracts for employment contain limits. Also, federal law makes limitations for certain occupations such as truck drivers.

Overtime Pay for Work More than 40 Hours Per Week

Subject to some legal exceptions for supervisory employees, for every hour worked more than 40 in a workweek, the employer is required to pay the employee at a rate not less than one and on-half times (1.5) the regular rate of pay.

What Can Be Taken from My Wages?

Generally, the following items can be deducted from you wages:

1. Taxes;
2. Wage garnishments like child support and judgments. Note: if you are being garnished for a judgment you should receive a notice that described how you can contest the garnishment. For example, if you are not able to pay your bills after the garnishment you can contest it in court; and
3. Other deductions like insurance, 401(k), pensions, etc.
4. The cost of uniforms or other work clothes, but only if the uniform does not indentify the business through a logo or company colors. Deductions may be allowed if the uniform is generic clothing such as a white shirt or khaki pants.

Generally, the following items cannot legally be deducted from your wages:

1. Cash shortages in common money till;
2. Losses due to breakage, damage, acceptance of bad checks, and default of customer credit except in certain limited cases;
3. Lost or stolen property unless certain conditions are met;
4. Tips;
5. Personal protective equipment in most cases; and
6. Moving costs except in certain cases

How Can My Wages Be Paid?

If you were hired after July 1, 2015, your employer may require direct deposit of your wages, but you are allowed to choose the bank or credit union. You may elect to not have direct deposit if you are charged for direct deposit, the costs of opening and keeping the account drops your pay below minimum wage or your union contract prohibits direct deposit.

An employer may pay wages on a debit card if:

1. The employee agrees in writing;
2. The funds are available to the employee on or before each pay day;
3. The employee is allowed access to all wages due without a fee or charge.

Regardless of the method of payment, an employer is required to provide a pay stub showing:

1. The number of hours the employee worked;
2. The wages earned by the employee; and
3. The deductions made from that paycheck.

Am I Required to Be Paid if I am Called for Jury Duty?

Neither Iowa, nor Federal law requires your employer to pay hourly non-exempt employees for jury duty. However, if you are a salaried worker, then wages may not be reduced as a result of absence due to jury duty. Keep in mind that all non-exempt hourly employees should be treated the same with regards to jury duty pay. An employer is allowed to change its policy if it communicates it clearly and consistently.

FMLA- Family Medical Leave Act

Eligibility- To be eligible for FMLA leave, an employee must work for a **covered employer** and:

- have worked for that employer for at least 12 months; and
- have worked at least 1,250 hours during the 12 months prior to the start of the FMLA leave; and,
- work at a location where at least 50 employees are employed at the location or within 75 miles of the location.

The FMLA is applicable to any employer in the private sector who is engaged in commerce or in any industry or activity affecting commerce, and who has **50 or more employees each working day** during at least 20 calendar weeks or more in the current or preceding calendar year. If your employer meets theses qualifications, then it is a **covered employer**.

All public agencies (state and local government) and local education agencies (schools) are covered. These employers do not need to meet the 50 employee test. Most federal employees are covered by Title II of FMLA and are subject to regulations issued by the Office of Personnel Management.

What Protection Does the FMLA Provide?- In order to be entitled to 12 week unpaid leave you must fall into one of the following categories, subject to some exceptions:

> (A) Because of the birth of a son or daughter of the employee and in order to care for such son or daughter.
>
> (B) Because of the placement of a son or daughter with the employee for adoption or foster care.
>
> (C) In order to care for the spouse, or a son, daughter, or parent, of the employee, if such spouse, son, daughter, or parent has a serious health condition.
>
> (D) Because of a serious health condition that makes the employee unable to perform the functions of the position of such employee.

A serious health condition is defined as:

An illness, injury, impairment, or physical or mental condition that involves:

> (A) inpatient care in a hospital, hospice, or residential medical care facility; or

(B) continuing treatment by a health care provider.

The term "health care provider" means:

> (A) a doctor of medicine or osteopathy who is authorized to practice medicine or surgery (as appropriate) by the State in which the doctor practices; or
>
> (B) any other person determined by the Secretary to be capable of providing health care services.

If all these items are met, then the employee may be entitled to 12 weeks of unpaid leave from work without being terminated. However, your employer may offer sick pay, STD (short term disability) benefits or other benefits that allow you to be paid during part of or all of the 12-week period. If the employer does not provide the 12 weeks as required, then you may have a cause of action against the employer. This is not designed to be an all-inclusive list of the steps which must be taken under the FMLA, in fact there may be other requirements which must be met. Therefore, each particular case should be analyzed under the FMLA and an attorney consulted regarding what to do.

Note: Yes, your employer can run your 12 weeks of FMLA time while you are off work recovering from a work injury. However, if they do end up firing you at the end of 12 weeks, you may have an employment law claim under the ADA or other employment laws described below.

ADA- Americans with Disabilities Act

The Americans With Disabilities Act (ADA) became effective on July 26, 1992, and was amended and made to apply more broadly effective January 1, 2009. The ADA's purpose is "to provide a clear and comprehensive national mandate for the elimination of discrimination against individuals with disabilities." The ADA prohibits employment discrimination by a covered entity against a disabled employee or job applicant who is qualified to perform the essential activities of the job. The prohibition against employment discrimination applies to hiring, termination, compensation, job advancement, and any other employment condition. A covered entity is defined by the act as "an employer, employment agency, labor organization, or joint labor-management committee . . which has 15 or more employees for each working day in each of 20 or more calendar weeks in the current or preceding calendar year, and any agent of such person."

If your employer is covered by the ADA, why would it matter? If you have an adverse employment action like being fired, demoted, not hired, etc. then you may want to investigate whether or not your employer or perspective employer has violated the ADA. Also, you may want to send a letter to your employer or perspective employer requesting an accommodation. The time limitations to do things in these cases can be very short so it makes sense to contact an employment law attorney concerning these matters before perhaps making a costly mistake.

If your employer is covered by the ADA, what do you have to prove? First of all, you have to provide that you have a disability under the ADA. These are very fact specific cases, and an attorney will likely need to review your medical records and meet with you to give his/her opinion as to whether or not you actually qualify, but generally the ADA defines disability as: "(A) a physical or mental impairment that substantially limits one or more of the major life activities of such individual; (B) a record of such an impairment; or (C) being regarded as having such an impairment." The following are to be considered when determining if there is a disability:

1. Disability is assessed without regard to the beneficial effects of any mitigating measures. (For example, diabetes is now analyzed as if the individual were not using insulin or other medications or techniques, so the drastic consequences of untreated diabetes may make a disability finding straightforward.)

2. For episodic conditions or those in remission, disability is assessed in the condition's active state.

3. Major life activities include the operation of a major bodily function. (This includes internal things, such as liver functioning in a person with hepatitis B, regardless of whether the condition has any impact on the person's external actions, such as working or eating.)

4. "Regarded as" is greatly expanded and requires only that the action is taken because of an impairment. The concepts of major life activity and substantial limitations are no longer relevant in regarded-as cases.

(**Note:** If you think you have been discriminated against because of a disability it is important that you seek legal advice as time deadlines can be very short and failing to timely file a claim can result in your case being forever barred).

Iowa and Federal Civil Rights Acts

Iowa Code Chapter 216 sets out the rights of employees and employers under the Iowa Civil Rights Act, which was originally passed in 1965, but has been amended throughout the years. The law also covers housing, public accommodation, education and obtaining credit for a loan, but we will only discus employment law in this book. The Iowa Civil Rights Act applies if the employer regularly employees 4 or more employees and family members of the employer do not count as employees.

The Federal Civil Rights act was passed in 1964 and also has been amended by Congress. It provides protection to employees if the employer has 15 or more employees. The Iowa Civil Rights Commission deals with Iowa claims and the EEOC- Equal Employment Opportunity Commission deals with federal claims. Often claims are "cross-filed" meaning that they are filed before both agencies. The state and federal laws are different, and you should consult with an attorney to determine what the best way is to pursue your potential claim.

The general basis of the law is that it shall be an unfair or a discriminatory practice for any person (company) to do any of the following:

a. To refuse to hire, accept, register, classify, or refer for employment, to discharge any employee, or to otherwise discriminate in employment against any applicant for employment or any employee because of the age, race, creed, color, sex, sexual orientation, gender identity, national origin, religion, or disability of such applicant or employee, unless based upon the nature of the occupation. If a person with a disability is qualified to perform a particular occupation, by reason of training or experience, the nature of that occupation shall not be the basis for exception to the unfair or discriminating practices prohibited by this subsection.

If you qualify for one of the above such as you are a woman for example, then you are considered a "protected class", but still are required to prove that the discrimination occurred because you are a woman for example.

Retaliation- It is also considered an unfair or discriminatory practice for any person (company) to:

Discriminate or retaliate against another person in any of the rights protected against discrimination by this chapter because such person has lawfully opposed any practice forbidden under this chapter, obeys the provisions of this chapter, or has filed a complaint, testified, or assisted in any proceeding under this chapter

Filing a Complaint- If you believe that you have been discriminated against and want to pursue the matter then you are required to file a complaint with either the Iowa Civil Rights Commission and/or the EEOC. The Iowa Civil Rights complaint form is available at: https://icrc.iowa.gov/file-complaint.

Time Limitations- Keep in mind that the time limit to file a complaint is generally 300 days after your have been discriminated against, but you should definitely not wait that long to file a complaint and/or contact an attorney about your discrimination.

ADEA- Age Discrimination In Employment Act

In 1967, Congress passed the ADEA- Age Discrimination in Employment Act. An employer (a person engaged in an industry affecting commerce) must have 20 or more employees for each working day in each of twenty or more calendar weeks (in the current or preceding calendar year) to be covered by the ADEA. An employee must be over age 40 to be covered by the ADEA (a "older employee").

The ADEA specifically prohibits the following:

1. Firing or refusing to hire employees based upon their age.
2. Denying benefits to "older employees".
3. Imposing involuntary retirement before age 70.
4. Asking a potential employee about their age for a purpose prohibited by the ADEA.

However, the ADEA does allow age restrictions in a limited number of circumstances like when age is shown to be a "bona fide occupational qualification". Also, the ADEA allows reduction of benefits based on age if the cost of providing the reduced benefits to older workers is the same as the cost of providing benefits to younger workers.

Complaints under the ADEA are filed with the EEOC and time limitations can be much shorter to file a complaint. These limits can be as short at 15 days from when you receive a notice after you speak with EEOC

Counselor. The Iowa Civil Rights Act also prohibits discrimination based upon age and you should speak with a qualified employment law attorney to decide where and when to file a complaint.

FLSA- Fair Labor Standards Act of 1938, as amended 29 U.S.C. 201, et seq.

The Act applies to enterprises that have employees who are engaged in interstate commerce, producing goods for interstate commerce, or handling, selling or working on goods or materials that have been moved in or produced for interstate commerce. For most firms, an annual dollar volume of business test of $500,000 applies (i.e., those enterprises under this dollar amount are not covered).

The following are covered by the Act regardless of their dollar volume of business: hospitals, institutions primarily engaged in the care of the sick, aged, mentally ill or disabled who reside on the premises; schools for children who are mentally or physically disabled or gifted; preschools, elementary and secondary schools and institutions of higher education; and federal, state and local government agencies.

Employees of firms that do not meet the $500,000 annual dollar volume test may be individually covered in any workweek in which they are individually engaged in interstate commerce, the production of goods for interstate commerce, or an activity which is closely related and directly essential to the production of such goods. Domestic service workers, such as day workers, housekeepers, chauffeurs, cooks, or full-time babysitters, are also covered if they receive at least $1,000 (1995) in cash wages from one employer in a calendar year, or if they work a total of more than 8 hours a week for one or more employers.

An enterprise that was covered by the Act on March 31, 1990, and that ceased to be covered because of the increase in the annual dollar volume test to $500,000, as required under the 1989 amendments to the Act, continues to be subject to the overtime pay, child labor and recordkeeping requirements of the Act.

What Protections Do the FLSA- Fair Labor Standards Act Provide?
Minimum Wage

The Act sets federal minimum wage at $7.25 per hour, but some states have increased this amount on their own. Iowa is not among the states that has increased minimum wage.

Under Iowa law, an employer is allowed to pay an "initial employment wage" of $6.35 per hour for the first 90 days and there are exceptions for seasonal workers and workers who primarily rely upon tips.

Prohibition of Wages Difference Based Solely Upon Being a Man or Woman

An employer is prohibited from paying wages to the opposite sex for jobs that require equal skill, effort and responsibility which are performed under similar working conditions except where payment is based upon:

a. a seniority system;

b. a merit system;

c. a system which measures earning by quantity or quality of production; or

d. a differential based on any other factor other than sex.

Health Insurance Enrollment

Employers with more than 200 full-time employees that offers employees enrollment in 1 or more health benefits plans are to automatically enroll new full-time employees in one of the plans offered (subject to any waiting period authorized by law) and to continue the enrollment of current employees in a health benefits plan offered through the employer. Any automatic enrollment program shall include adequate notice and the opportunity for an employee to opt out of any coverage the individual or employee were automatically enrolled in.

COBRA- Continuation of Health Insurance Coverage

What does COBRA do? COBRA provides certain former employees, retirees, spouses, former spouses, and dependent children the right to temporary continuation of health coverage at group rates. This coverage, however, is only available when coverage is lost due to certain specific events. Group health coverage for COBRA participants is usually more expensive than health coverage for active employees, since usually the employer pays a part of the premium for active employees while COBRA participants generally pay the entire premium themselves.

COBRA rates may be higher than other available plans so you should check with a local insurance agent and/or www.Healthcare.gov to see if you qualify for a less expensive option.

Who is entitled to benefits under COBRA? There are three elements to qualifying for COBRA benefits. COBRA establishes specific criteria for plans, qualified beneficiaries, and qualifying events:

Plan Coverage - Group health plans for employers with **20 or more employees** on more than 50 percent of its typical business days in the previous calendar year are subject to COBRA. Both full and part-time employees are counted to determine whether a plan is subject to COBRA. Each part-time employee counts as a fraction of an employee, with the fraction equal to the number of hours that the part-time employee worked divided by the hours an employee must work to be considered full time.

Qualified Beneficiaries - A qualified beneficiary generally is an individual covered by a group health plan on the day before a qualifying event who is either an employee, the employee's spouse, or an employee's dependent child. In certain cases, a retired employee, the retired employee's spouse, and the retired employee's dependent children may be qualified beneficiaries. In addition, any child born to or placed for adoption with a covered employee during the period of COBRA coverage is considered a qualified beneficiary. Agents, independent contractors, and directors who participate in the group health plan may also be qualified beneficiaries.

Qualifying Events - Qualifying events are certain events that would cause an individual to lose health coverage. The type of qualifying event will determine who the qualified beneficiaries are and the amount of time that a plan must offer the health coverage to them under COBRA. A plan, at its discretion, may provide longer periods of continuation coverage.

Qualifying Events for Employees:

- Voluntary or involuntary termination of employment for reasons other than gross misconduct
- Reduction in the number of hours of employment

Qualifying Events for Spouses:

- Voluntary or involuntary termination of the covered employee's employment for any reason other than gross misconduct
- Reduction in the hours worked by the covered employee

- Covered employee's becoming entitled to Medicare
- Divorce or legal separation of the covered employee
- Death of the covered employee

Qualifying Events for Dependent Children:

- Loss of dependent child status under the plan rules
- Voluntary or involuntary termination of the covered employee's employment for any reason other than gross misconduct
- Reduction in the hours worked by the covered employee
- Covered employee's becoming entitled to Medicare
- Divorce or legal separation of the covered employee
- Death of the covered employee

How does a person become eligible for COBRA continuation coverage? To be eligible for COBRA coverage, you must have been enrolled in your employer's health plan when you worked, and the health plan must continue to be in effect for active employees. COBRA continuation coverage is available upon the occurrence of a qualifying event that would, except for the COBRA continuation coverage, cause an individual to lose his or her health care coverage.

What process must individuals follow to elect COBRA continuation coverage? Employers must notify plan administrators of a qualifying event within 30 days after an employee's death, termination, reduced hours of employment or entitlement to Medicare. A qualified beneficiary must notify the plan administrator of a qualifying event within 60 days after divorce or legal separation or a child's ceasing to be covered as a dependent under plan rules.

How long after a qualifying event do I have to elect COBRA coverage? Qualified beneficiaries must be given an election period during which each qualified beneficiary may choose whether to elect COBRA coverage. Each qualified beneficiary may independently elect COBRA coverage. A covered employee or the covered employee's spouse may elect COBRA coverage on behalf of all other qualified beneficiaries. A parent or legal guardian may elect on behalf of a minor child. Qualified beneficiaries must be given at least 60 days for the election. This period is measured from the later of the coverage loss date or the date the COBRA election notice is provided by the employer or plan administrator. The election notice must be provided in person or by first class mail within 14 days after the plan administrator receives notice that a qualifying event has occurred.

How do I file a COBRA claim for benefits? Health plan rules must explain how to obtain benefits and must include written procedures for processing claims. Claims procedures must be described in the Summary Plan Description. You should submit a claim for benefits in accordance with the plan's rules for filing claims. If the claim is denied, you must be given notice of the denial in writing generally within 90 days after the claim is filed. The notice should state the reasons for the denial, any additional information needed to support the claim, and procedures for appealing the denial.

You will have at least 60 days to appeal a denial and you must receive a decision on the appeal generally within 60 days after that.

Contact the plan administrator for more information on filing a claim for benefits. Complete plan rules are available from employers or benefits offices. There can be charges up to 25 cents a page for copies of plan rules.

Can individuals qualify for longer periods of COBRA continuation coverage? Yes, disability can extend the 18 month period of continuation coverage for a qualifying event that is a termination of employment or reduction of hours. To qualify for additional months of COBRA continuation coverage, the qualified beneficiary must:

- Have a ruling from the Social Security Administration that he or she became disabled within the first 60 days of COBRA continuation coverage

- Send the plan a copy of the Social Security ruling letter within 60 days of receipt, but prior to expiration of the 18-month period of coverage

If these requirements are met, the entire family qualifies for an additional 11 months of COBRA continuation coverage. Plans can charge 150% of the premium cost for the extended period of coverage.

Is a divorced spouse entitled to COBRA coverage from their former spouses' group health plan? Under COBRA, participants, covered spouses and dependent children may continue their plan coverage for a limited time when they would otherwise lose coverage due to a particular event, such as divorce (or legal separation). A covered employee's spouse who would lose coverage due to a divorce may elect continuation coverage under the plan for a maximum of 36 months. A qualified beneficiary must notify the plan administrator of a qualifying event within

60 days after divorce or legal separation. After being notified of a divorce, the plan administrator must give notice, generally within 14 days, to the qualified beneficiary of the right to elect COBRA continuation coverage.

Divorced spouses may call their plan administrator or the EBSA Toll-Free number, 1.866.444.EBSA (3272) if they have questions about COBRA continuation coverage or their rights under ERISA.

If I waive COBRA coverage during the election period, can I still get coverage at a later date? If a qualified beneficiary waives COBRA coverage during the election period, he or she may revoke the waiver of coverage before the end of the election period. A beneficiary may then elect COBRA coverage. Then, the plan need only provide continuation coverage beginning on the date the waiver is revoked.

Under COBRA, what benefits must be covered? Qualified beneficiaries must be offered coverage identical to that available to similarly situated beneficiaries who are not receiving COBRA coverage under the plan (generally, the same coverage that the qualified beneficiary had immediately before qualifying for continuation coverage). A change in the benefits under the plan for the active employees will also apply to qualified beneficiaries. Qualified beneficiaries must be allowed to make the same choices given to non-COBRA beneficiaries under the plan, such as during periods of open enrollment by the plan.

When does COBRA coverage begin? COBRA coverage begins on the date that health care coverage would otherwise have been lost by reason of a qualifying event.

How long does COBRA coverage last? COBRA establishes required periods of coverage for continuation health benefits. A plan, however, may provide longer periods of coverage beyond those required by COBRA. COBRA beneficiaries generally are eligible for group coverage during a maximum of 18 months for qualifying events due to employment termination or reduction of hours of work. Certain qualifying events, or a second qualifying event during the initial period of coverage, may permit a beneficiary to receive a maximum of 36 months of coverage.

Coverage begins on the date that coverage would otherwise have been lost by reason of a qualifying event and will end at the end of the maximum period. It may end earlier if:

- Premiums are not paid on a timely basis
- The employer ceases to maintain any group health plan
- After the COBRA election, coverage is obtained with another employer group health plan that does not contain any exclusion or limitation with respect to any pre-existing condition of such beneficiary. However, if other group health coverage is obtained prior to the COBRA election, COBRA coverage may not be discontinued, even if the other coverage continues after the COBRA election.
- After the COBRA election, a beneficiary becomes entitled to Medicare benefits. However, if Medicare is obtained prior to COBRA election, COBRA coverage may not be discontinued, even if the other coverage continues after the COBRA election.

Although COBRA specifies certain periods of time that continued health coverage must be offered to qualified beneficiaries, COBRA does not prohibit plans from offering continuation health coverage that goes beyond the COBRA periods.

Some plans allow participants and beneficiaries to convert group health coverage to an individual policy. If this option is generally available from the plan, a qualified beneficiary who pays for COBRA coverage must be given the option of converting to an individual policy at the end of the COBRA continuation coverage period. The option must be given to enroll in a conversion health plan within 180 days before COBRA coverage ends. The premium for a conversion policy may be more expensive than the premium of a group plan, and the conversion policy may provide a lower level of coverage. The conversion option, however, is not available if the beneficiary ends COBRA coverage before reaching the end of the maximum period of COBRA coverage.

Who pays for COBRA coverage? Beneficiaries may be required to pay for COBRA coverage. The premium cannot exceed 102 percent of the cost to the plan for similarly situated individuals who have not incurred a qualifying event, including both the portion paid by employees and any portion paid by the employer before the qualifying event, plus 2 percent for administrative costs.

For qualified beneficiaries receiving the 11 month disability extension of coverage, the premium for those additional months may be increased to 150 percent of the plan's total cost of coverage.

COBRA premiums may be increased if the costs to the plan increase but generally must be fixed in advance of each 12-month premium cycle. The plan must allow you to pay premiums on a monthly basis if you ask to do so, and the plan may allow you to make payments at other intervals (weekly or quarterly).

The initial premium payment must be made within 45 days after the date of the COBRA election by the qualified beneficiary. Payment generally must cover the period of coverage from the date of COBRA election retroactive to the date of the loss of coverage due to the qualifying event. Premiums for successive periods of coverage are due on the date stated in the plan with a minimum 30-day grace period for payments. Payment is considered to be made on the date it is sent to the plan.

If premiums are not paid by the first day of the period of coverage, the plan has the option to cancel coverage until payment is received and then reinstate coverage retroactively to the beginning of the period of coverage.

If the amount of the payment made to the plan is made in error but is not significantly less than the amount due, the plan is required to notify you of the deficiency and grant a reasonable period (for this purpose, 30 days is considered reasonable) to pay the difference. The plan is not obligated to send monthly premium notices.

COBRA beneficiaries remain subject to the rules of the plan and therefore must satisfy all costs related to co-payments and deductibles, and are subject to catastrophic and other benefit limits.

If I elect COBRA, how much do I pay? When you were an active employee, your employer may have paid all or part of your group health premiums. Under COBRA, as a former employee no longer receiving benefits, you will usually pay the entire premium amount, that is, the portion of the premium that you paid as an active employee and the amount of the contribution made by your employer. In addition, there may be a 2 percent administrative fee.

Since it is likely that there will be a lapse of a month or more between the date of layoff and the time you make the COBRA election decision, you may have to pay health premiums retroactively-from the time of separation from the company. The first premium, for instance, will cover the entire time since your last day of employment with your former employer.

You should also be aware that it is your responsibility to pay for COBRA coverage even if you do not receive a monthly statement.

Can I receive COBRA benefits while on FMLA leave? The Family and Medical Leave Act, effective August 5, 1993, requires an employer to maintain coverage under any group health plan for an employee on FMLA leave under the same conditions coverage would have been provided if the employee had continued working. Coverage provided under the FMLA is not COBRA coverage, and FMLA leave is not a qualifying event under COBRA. A COBRA qualifying event may occur, however, when an employer's obligation to maintain health benefits under FMLA ceases, such as when an employee notifies an employer of his or her intent not to return to work.

What If I Think My FLSA Rights Have Been Violated?

Section 15(a)(3) of the FLSA states that it is a violation for any person to "discharge or in any other manner discriminate against any employee because such employee has filed any complaint or instituted or caused to be instituted any proceeding under or related to this Act, or has testified or is about to testify in any such proceeding, or has served or is about to serve on an industry committee."

Employees can make their complaints in writing or orally and are protected either way. Complaints made to the Wage and Hour Division are protected, and most courts have ruled that internal complaints to an employer are also protected.

Any employee who is "discharged or in any other manner discriminated against" because, for instance, he or she has filed a complaint or cooperated in an investigation, may file a retaliation complaint with the Wage and Hour Division or may file a private cause of action seeking appropriate remedies including, but not limited to, employment, reinstatement, lost wages, and an additional equal amount as liquidated damages.

OSHA- Occupational Safety and Health Administration

In general, coverage of the Act extends to all employers and their employees in the 50 states, the District of Columbia, Puerto Rico, and all other territories under Federal Government jurisdiction. Coverage is provided either directly by federal OSHA or through an OSHA-approved state program.

As defined by the Act, an employer is any "person engaged in a business affecting commerce who has employees but does not include the United States or any State or political subdivision of a State."

The following are not covered under the Act:

- Self-employed persons;
- Farms at which only immediate members of the farm employer's family are employed; and
- Working conditions regulated by other federal agencies under other federal laws.

If you feel that there has been a OSHA violation that you would like to report, you can contact either the United Statement Department of Labor at www.OSHA.gov or Iowa OSHA Enforcement at 1-800-562-4692 or 515-242-5870 or go to www.IowaWorkForce.org to file a OSHA complaint.

Do I Have a Right to Get My Employment File?

Iowa Code Section 91B.1 provides the law for the rights that you have to your employment file. Generally, yes you have the right to obtain a copy of your file from your current employer including, but not limited to your performance evaluations, disciplinary records and other information concerning employer-employee relations. There are some requirements, and your request is subject to the following:

a. The employer and employee shall agree on the time the employee may have access to the employee's personnel file, and a representative of the employer may be present.

b. An employee shall not have access to employment references written for the employee.

c. An employer may charge a reasonable fee for each page of a copy made by the employer for an employee of an item in the employee's personnel file. For purposes of this paragraph, "reasonable fee" means an amount equivalent to an amount charged per page for copies made by a commercial copying business.

(Note: if you are no longer employed, your employer may refuse to voluntarily provide you with a copy of your employment file based upon the following court decision. Dunn v. Dubuque Glass Co., Inc., 870 F. Supp.2d 654 (N.D. Iowa 2012) which found employees were no longer employees when they requested their employment records, precluding their claims that employer violated Iowa statutes stating that an employee was entitled to access to the employee's personnel file, and requiring an employer to furnish certain information in response to an employee's request for information.

Can Your Employer Ask For a Drug or Alcohol Test?

Iowa Code Section 730.5 was passed in 1987, amended in 1998 and provides specific requirements for when an employer can seek a drug or alcohol test of an employee. The law has been amended a few times, but only applies to private sector employers and does not apply if testing is required under federal law. The first requirement is that the employer must have a written policy and employees are to be provided with a copy of the policy. Further, the policy is to be available for review by you as the employee. The policy may or may not include alcohol testing, but if it does it must specify the threshold for alcohol concentration which may not be below .02.

In addition to a written policy, employers are required to have an "awareness program" to inform employees of the dangers of drug and alcohol use in the workplace. Also, if they want to test employees, they are to have an EAP (employee assistance program) or "maintain a resource file of alcohol and other drug abuse programs certified by the Iowa Department of Public Health".

If you have applied for a job, your prospective employee may require you to submit to testing before you are hired for a job.

If your current employer asks you for a drug or alcohol test keep the following in mind:

1. The employer is to pay all actual costs for the testing.
2. Testing is to occur before, during or after a regular work period.

3. You are to be paid for the time you are required to take the test.

4. The employer must provide transportation or pay reasonable costs if the testing is done offsite.

5. Your employer is allowed to choose the type of test to be used either urine, saliva or breath. A blood test is only allowed when the test was conducted as a part of the medical care and treatment following a work injury.

6. The testing is to be performed under sanitary conditions and with regards to your privacy.

7. Your employer is required to send you the results of the test by certified mail including notifying you of the right to request and obtain a second test.

Who is Allowed to Be Tested Randomly? Random drug testing can be conducted on all workers at a certain site, all full-time active workers at a certain site or all employees of a particular site who are in a group of employees who are in a safety-sensitive position. The selection of who to test is to be done by an independent company separate from the employer and based upon a computer random number generator.

Other Drug Testing-

1. If you sustain a work injury accident (should not apply to a cumulative or repetitive injury) or there is property damage of more than $1,000. If the medical provider takes a blood test as part of your care and treatment, that test may be used against you.

2. If the employer has a reasonable suspicion that you are under the influence of drugs and/or alcohol

3. Testing is required by federal law.

4. Testing can also be requested during and after completion of drug or alcohol rehabilitation.

Other Information- You can be suspended with or without pay pending the outcome of a test. If the test is negative, then you should be reinstated and receive back pay. Regardless, you should receive the test results in writing. If your initial test is positive, then the employer must confirm the test through a laboratory certified by the United States Department of Health and Human Services. If the test is confirmed positive, then you have the right to obtain a 2nd confirmatory test at your expense within 7 days. A confirmed positive test can result in your suspension, termination or not being hired if the testing is part of your application process. However, if you are employed and your employer has a written policy that allows for rehabilitation, then no adverse action should be taken against you if you comply with the requirements and successfully complete rehabilitation.

If your employer has 50 or more employees and you have worked for the employer for at least 12 of the last 18 months, then their written policy for alcohol rehabilitation may require your employer to pay for part of your treatment and keep your job for you after treatment.

Write any questions, comments, or concerns that you may have in the space below:

Page left blank intentionally.

Chapter 11

What If I Have Been Fired or Quit? Filing for Unemployment

As discussed in the workers' compensation chapter, if you are receiving weekly workers' compensation checks and are fired, then there is a right and wrong time to file for unemployment. Generally, if you are fired then you should file for unemployment. You can start the process to file your claim online at www.iowaworkforce.org/ui/file1.htm or go to your local IowaWORKS Center with 15 locations across the state including Des Moines, Cedar Rapids, Sioux City, Waterloo, Davenport, Dubuque, Spencer, Decorah, Fort Dodge, Ottumwa, Mason City, Creston, Council Bluffs, Carroll and Burlington.

The basic requirements to qualify for Iowa unemployment benefits are:

1. You have enough work credits to qualify which generally means you have worked and earned wages in work covered by unemployment insurance for the past 15 to 18 months.
2. You are totally or partially unemployed
3. You were terminated from your job without cause, but did not commit "misconduct" <u>or</u> you left your job with "good cause" attributable to the employer
4. You are ready, willing, and able to work
5. You are actively seeking work applying for at least 4 jobs per week and documenting your job search efforts

Termination- If your employer terminated you then it is your employer's burden to prove "misconduct" in order for you to be denied unemployment benefits. "Misconduct" includes committing an indictable criminal act while working (for example, driving drunk while working, assaults, etc), actions which show wrongful intent or evil design, intentional and substantial disregard of the employer's interests or of the employee's duties and obligations to the employer. For example, excessive unexcused absenteeism is an intentional disregard of the duty owed by the claimant to the employer and shall be considered misconduct except for illness or other reasonable grounds for which the employee was absent and that were properly reported to the employer.

You may also receive unemployment if you take a leave of absence because of illness, injury, or pregnancy upon the advice of a licensed and practicing physician. Upon recovery, when recovery is certified by a licensed and practicing physician, you return and offer to perform the prior job for the employer, but no suitable, comparable work was available then you may qualify for unemployment. Keep in mind that you may also be protected by the FMLA- Family Medical Leave Act.

Voluntary Quit- If you quit your job and can prove it is due to "good cause" attributable to the employer then you may also receive unemployment benefits. Examples of "good cause" would be:

a. A significant change in your contract of hire like changing the times and days you are to work;

b. Relocation of your spouse by the military;

c. For the sole purpose of taking care of your immediate family member who is injured or ill and if after your member of the family recovered you immediately returned to work and offered to perform work which was declined by your employer;

d. You leave employment based upon the advice of a licensed and practicing physician because of an illness or pregnancy, you immediately notify your employer of the need for your absence and when you recovered you are not offered work. For example, if you have a medical condition caused or aggravated by work making it impossible to continue to work within your work restrictions and your job is not changed or modified after you provide notice to your employer;

e. You leave work for no more than 10 working days for compelling personal reasons that you tell your employer about before leaving and immediately after the your personal reason ends you offer to work and your regular or comparable work is not available; and

f. For more "good cause" reasons see Iowa Code Annotated Section 96.5.

<u>What if My Employer Contests My Case?</u> If your employer does not think that you should receive unemployment benefits, then they will file an objection. The matter will then be set for a fact-finding interview. There are some cases where, even though the employer does not file an objection, Iowa Workforce Development may decide to still hold a fact-finding interview. You should receive a written notice of the interview and should read the paperwork you receive very carefully. Generally, you will be required to call Iowa Workforce and provide them with the number to call you for the interview. Failing to participate in the interview may result in your not receiving benefits because the person conducting the interview will only hear the employer's side of the story. You are allowed to submit a written statement, but we recommend that you participate in the interview.

What If I am Denied or My Employer Appeals? After the fact-finding interview, you will receive a written notice indicating whether you qualify for benefits. If your claim is denied, the next step would be to file an appeal if you want to contest it. There are very short time deadlines (generally 10 days) to file an appeal and it is important that you read the instructions about how to file an appeal, etc. Appeals can be filed online at https://www.iowaworkforcedevelopment.gov/ui-appeal . If you received benefits, but the employer disagrees, they can file an appeal. Either party can request an in person appeal hearing, but the vast majority are done by telephone.

Do I Need an Attorney? It is up to you if you hire an attorney or not, but if you are not experienced with the process, handling it on your own can be risky and cause problems. If you have a work injury and/or employment law claim it is very important that you contact an attorney for help as the unemployment law case can have a big impact on your other legal claims. Sometimes your employer will hire an attorney to defend them in the unemployment law case you have filed which can put you at a disadvantage without your own attorney.

Administrative Hearing- If there is an appeal of the findings from the fact-finding interview you will receive a Notice of Appeal and Hearing document. It will contain the time and date and then the matter will be set for a phone or in person hearing before an administrative law judge. Either party can request an in person hearing when an appeal is filed, but the vast majority of the time the hearings are done by phone. It is important that once you receive the notice of hearing that you read the requirements which include calling into Iowa Workforce to participate in the hearing, mailing or faxing any documents (formally called exhibits) that you want the judge to review and sending a copy of the documents to the employer. Also, if you have witnesses that you want to appear at the hearing you will need to follow the proper procedure explained in the Notice of Appeal and Hearing.

Tips For Hearings

Whether you are participating in the initial fact-finding interview or the administrative hearing, it is important to keep some things in mind:

1. Be polite during the process. The hearing officers and judges usually have 10 or more hearings per day and even if they are not polite to you, you should be respectful and polite to them. They are the ones making the decision and rudeness will not get you very far.

2. Know your facts and be organized. If the hearing officer or judge asks you when you started working, when your job ended, how your job ended, etc. have the information in front of you. Make sure any documents you want considered are sent to Iowa Workforce and the employer more than three days prior to the hearing to prevent delays.

3. Only talk when you have permission from the hearing officer or judge and never interrupt the judge or other side while they are talking. If you have an administrative hearing, it will be recorded and later on a transcript may be ordered which usually requires a court reporter to create a transcript of everything that was said which is why only one person should talk at time.

4. During the administrative hearing know when to ask questions and when to make statements. The judge will give you the opportunity to ask questions of the employer's witnesses called cross-examination, but that is not the time to make statements about your case. You can ask questions

like "would you agree that I had no attendance problems?", but you should not give statements when it is your turn to cross-examine witnesses. A good way to tell the difference is to remember a question is seeking information and a statement is giving information.

5. Have a good phone connection, be in a quiet place and speak clearly. It will be frustrating to all parties if they cannot hear you or there is background noise.

Employment Appeal Board- If one party does not like the administrative law judge decision, then an appeal can be filed to the unemployment appeal board. The decision will have instructions about how to file a further appeal, but usually the appeal has to be filed within 15 days from the mailing date. Generally, no further testimony or evidence will be allowed, but there are specific requirements about what should be in the appeal notice. The appeals board will usually accept briefs written by the parties at a later date.

Judicial Review- If one party disagrees with the decision of the Employment Appeal Board, then a petition can be filed in district court for judicial review. Generally, the petition must be filed within 30 days of the Appeals Board's decision. We would encourage you promptly contact an attorney if you are considering filing for judicial review and there are specific requirements for doing so.

Other Items- If you do qualify for unemployment benefits it will usually take 2 to 3 weeks after you file your claim before you receive your first check. If there are appeals, it can take much longer. The amount of the wages you earned in your "base period" will determine your weekly benefit amount and how much you can receive. A base period is the first four out of five complete quarters before your unemployment claim was filed. The most you can receive is 26 weeks or 1/3 of your total base-period wages, whichever is less. There can be unemployment extensions depending upon state and federal laws passed. Keep in mind that the following items are generally 100% deductible from your unemployment benefits: vacation pay, holiday pay, severance pay, and TTD- temporary total workers' compensation disability benefits.

Severance Packages- If you are offered a severance package and you sign it, those benefits are sometimes, but not always, deductible from unemployment insurance benefits. Therefore, before signing any severance package it is a good idea to get some legal advice from an attorney.

Write any questions, comments, or concerns that you may have in the space below:

Page left blank intentionally.

CHAPTER 12

I Think That I Am Disabled. Should I File for Social Security Disability?

The answer to this question is that it depends on the specific facts of your case. Filing too early can sometimes be a mistake that can cost you thousands of dollars. Therefore, if you are considering filing you should call our office at 641-792-3595 and we can discuss your specific facts. However, here is an overview of the Social Security disability laws.

Types of Benefits Available

There are two types of Disability benefits through Social Security.

- Benefits from Social Security Disability Insurance
- Benefits from Supplemental Security Income.

Both types are for individuals under age 65 (Supplemental Security Income benefits can continue after retirement in some situations), who meet the medical criteria for Disability. The difference in benefits depends on an individual's work history.

SSDI – Social Security Disability Insurance

In order to qualify for SSDI, an individual must have paid enough into Social Security through their taxes. This is judged by financial quarters. The number of quarters you must have paid in varies depending on your age at the time of disability. But generally, an individual must have paid into SSA- Social Security Administration for at least 20 quarters, or 5 years of taxes within the last 10 years prior to disability. The more an individual pays in through their taxes, the more money they financially qualify for. As a result, everyone's monthly benefit rate is different. Social Security Disability Insurance benefit amounts may be affected by certain types of public disability benefits, discussed in more detail later on.

SSI – Supplemental Security Income

For individuals who have not worked enough quarters to financially qualify for SSDI, SSI provides some income when you otherwise medically qualify for Social Security benefits. SSI is more limited than SSDI in that it may consider income coming into an adult individual's household in determining financial eligibility. So if you have a spouse who lives with you and works full time, they may earn too much income for your household for you to qualify for SSI benefits. There are strict financial qualifications for SSI benefits, which is why it is important to discuss SSI benefits with an experienced attorney to find out more.

Who Qualifies for Social Security Disability Benefits?

Individuals with limitations who can no longer earn substantial income must qualify for benefits both financially, as well as medically. The medical requirements are addressed below. There are several qualifications an individual must fulfill to be considered disabled and qualify for benefits by Social Security. These qualifications are addressed in a five-step sequential evaluation process by Social Security. An individual seeking Disability benefits must meet these criteria in order to be found disabled.

What are the 5 Steps in Evaluating a Successful Social Security Disability Claim?

1. Are you engaging in substantial gainful activity?

This question asks whether you are currently working, or earning income, and if so, how much? According to SSA, you can continue to work and gain a small amount of income while being considered disabled, and still be eligible for Social Security Disability Insurance (SSDI) benefits. But the income threshold is low. As of 2015, an individual can earn roughly $1,090 gross per month without engaging in substantial gainful activity. (Note: this amount can change every year and is higher for blind individuals at $1,820 gross per month for 2015) However, keep in mind that the amount you earn each month can partially offset your amount of monthly Disability benefits.

If you are currently working and are concerned that you may be too close to making over the threshold, then you should try your best to increase your work hours! It is always better to work than to try for disability benefits.

However, if your impairments limit you from working near full time, then you should consider pursuing a claim for Social Security Disability benefits.

2. **Do you have a medically severe impairment?**

The second step of the evaluation process appears to be a very high standard, but it not as high as it may sound. Medically severe impairments are defined by the Social Security Administration and do not include medical conditions that cause only slight and/or temporary problems. Impairments can be considered medically severe, but if they are not expected to last 12 months or longer, or end in death, then they generally will not qualify.

3. **Do your limitations meet criteria within SSA's listing of impairments?**

Social Security has a listing of specific impairments, and the very narrow set of criteria an individual must meet in order to medically qualify for Disability benefits. This set of criteria is very specialized, and many individuals who medically qualify for Disability benefits do not directly meet these criteria. For more information you can look at the Adult Listings at: www.ssa.gov/disability/professionals/bluebook.

The Social Security Administration is required to move onto step 4 if the individual cannot be considered medically disabled under the listing of impairments.

4. **Can you resume any work you have performed within the last 15 years?**

Social Security will look at your past relevant work history which is defined as the work you have performed for a

significant period of time within the last 15 years. From this, it will use experts to determine whether or not your impairments keep you from performing the least taxing of your previous jobs within the last 15 years.
If an individual is found not to be able to perform any of their past relevant work, then Social Security must move onto step 5.

5. **Is there a sufficient amount of other work you can perform, considering your age, education and transferable skills?**

The final step in the evaluation process considers whether an individual can perform any other work that exists in the national economy (in sufficient quantity), given the individual's age, educational history and transferable skills. If the individual is found not to be able to complete any other work, then they will be determined to be medically disabled within the standard established by Social Security.

When to Apply for Benefits

The Social Security Administration recognizes that an individual may need access to financial benefits when they have an illness or injury which is significant enough to keep them from engaging in substantial gainful activity, and is expected to either result in death, or impairments lasting at least 12 months. This does not mean that you must wait 12 months after you stop working to apply for Social Security, in order to discover whether or not you are eligible. It merely means that your physician must have diagnosed you with an impairment that is predicted to last at least that length of time.

Impairments come in many forms. There are physical impairments and mental impairments. Physical impairments tend to prevent the individual from being able to perform basic physical activities to some degree of severity. Many physical impairments will inhibit your ability to bend, lift, twist, stoop, crouch, crawl, kneel, stand, walk, sit, reach, handle, grasp, carry, etc. Mental impairments tend to keep an individual from engaging in everyday activities. These can include the ability to: go out in public, interact with others, perform basic arithmetic and other cognitive skills, interact appropriately with co-workers and/or supervisors, etc.

These impairments can be varied, depending on the nature of the illness or injury the individual suffers from. As a result, it is essential to the success of a case to have an experienced representative who can assess which impairments, and to what degree of severity, will need to be focused on in order to find an individual disabled.

Note: If you have been hurt at work, if you are either represented by an attorney or are considering hiring an attorney, you should contact your attorney prior to applying for Social Security disability benefits as it may have a significant impact on your workers' compensation case.

How to Apply

There are two different ways to apply for Social Security Disability benefits. The first is to gather the information you will need in order to apply, such as: work history information; information about your medical care providers; education history; military history; and other important information; and apply electronically through the Social Security Administration's website, www.SSA.gov.

After this is done, the local field office will contact you for a telephone interview regarding your claim. The second way to apply is to call your field office and schedule an appointment to speak with them and file the application. These initial conferences, either by telephone or in person, are designed to get information from you that is needed to process your claim, such as what medical providers you have seen and when. As part of the process, you will be required to sign medical release forms allowing the Social Security Administration access to your medical records. This allows them to obtain copies of your medical records in order to make a determination on your medical eligibility.

Our Social Security Disability book discusses the above along with going into more detail about the claims process once you apply. We recommend that you at least request our book and talk to a qualified Social Security Disability attorney before applying as he/she will be able to give you their opinions about your case and may be able to speed the process up. Just call 641-792-3595 and ask for a copy of our Social Security Disability book and we will send it to you right away at no cost. An attorney knows how the system works and what the Social Security Administration is looking for when evaluating cases and determining who is disabled. The process can take from 6 months to several years and you may or may not be successful. If we accept your Social Security Disability case, then you are not required to pay a retainer or any up-front fees. We only get paid an attorney fee if we are successful in getting you disability and then it is limited to 25% of the past-due back benefits or $6,000 whichever is lower.

Write any questions, comments, or concerns that you may have in the space below:

Page left blank intentionally.

Chapter 13

Internet and Social Media- Facebook

Facebook in Litigation- If you have a case that is eventually litigated, then you will likely be required in your case to produce pictures, documents, messages, etc. that you have posted or received on social media sites like Facebook, etc.

My recommendation is for you to disable any and all social media sites that you have while this matter is pending. In our technology society, this information can be found by defendants and if they find something that they can use against you, they will.

> **FACT**- Courts have ordered people to produce their Facebook and other social media pages to the other side in the case.
>
> **FACT**- Evidence from Facebook and other social media pages has been admitted in Court and used against people making claims.
>
> **FACT**- Every defense lawyer has a law clerk on Facebook who is looking for information about you including profiles, pictures, posts, etc.

Here are some steps can you take to protect yourself:

1. Do not put information on social network web pages or other internet pages, send emails or texts about your case, injuries, or anything else that could potentially damage your case.

2. Take a critical eye to your social media sites to see if there is anything you would not want the other side to see. Remember that the other side will not know the context of your photos or comments. They won't know if you had to take extra pain medication the next day after you did something.

3. Check your privacy settings. Most sites allow you to block certain people altogether from seeing that you even are on the site. Block the opposing lawyer and email addresses ending with the name of the firm (for example @AhlersLaw.com). Keep in mind, however, that there will be law students and others whose names you won't know, so this is not foolproof.

4. Search for your name in the search field to see what comes up and make sure it is acceptable.

5. While you are at it, do the same thing on Google and YouTube. Make whatever adjustments are necessary.

6. Don't accept friend requests or answer emails through social medical from people you do not know. For example, on Facebook if you send a message, you grant the receiver access to your profile for a certain number of days. This is a common device to get access to your profile. Keep in mind that because of the lawsuit process, the opposing legal team knows a lot about you and could send you an email that might make you think you know each other. **If you are in doubt about whether or not your pages are acceptable, then chances are they are not.**

Chapter 14

Do You Really Need An Attorney In Your Case?

You definitely do not need an attorney for every injury case. For example, our office will not accept your case if your injuries are minor. Also, in car accident cases we will not accept you case if there was little or no damage to your vehicle. Why would we not handle these cases? First of all, in small cases the attorney fee and costs might leave little or nothing for you after your medical bills are paid which would not be fair to you. Also, these cases would take time away from the more significant cases that we handle. However, Iowans who have sustained serious personal injuries are beginning to realize that the insurance company is not there to help them with the case and that they should consider having someone on their side.

What Are the Benefits of Hiring an Attorney?

- You will have someone on your side fighting for you, protecting your rights, and explaining how the legal system works.

- Relieve your stress of dealing with the insurance company. Also, our experience in dealing with insurance companies will help ensure that you receive the full value of your case.

- Take away the pressure of collection agencies and medical providers calling about your medical bills as they will be directed to contact us.

- If your health insurance plan is <u>not</u> a self-funded ERISA plan, then you can charge the plan an attorney fee which goes back to you as our client. For example, if you have $15,000 in medical expenses paid by your health insurance plan, then if you have an attorney involved you only must pay the insurance company back $10,000 and the additional $5,000 goes to you. If you do not have an attorney involved, then the entire $15,000 goes to the health insurance company. If it is a self-funded ERISA plan we will negotiate with them, and often they will accept a substantial reduction. This increases the amount of money you receive.

- Trial Experience. If your case is not able to be settled, you will have a trial lawyer working hard to achieve the best possible verdict.

When Should You Hire an Attorney?

· Serious Injuries- If you have sustained serious personal injuries requiring surgery or other significant medical treatment. Before you make a potential mistake in your case you should have a qualified attorney on your side to help you through the process. (Hint: There are many issues involving unemployment law. For example, if you are fired and have been hurt at work there is a right and wrong time to apply for unemployment benefits. You need an attorney that can also help you through the unemployment process because it can have a significant impact upon your injury claim). The earlier you hire a qualified attorney to help you, the less likely that you will make a mistake that could cost you thousands of dollars. Keep in mind that if you are currently receiving weekly benefits, the attorney you hire should **not** take any percentage of your current benefits and most will not require you to pay a retainer or any up-front fees.

· Permanent Injury- If it did not appear that your injuries were serious at first, but after you are done treating you receive a permanent impairment rating and/or permanent restrictions or if you still have ongoing pain or limitations then you should talk to a qualified injury attorney to find-out if you should compensation for your permanent injuries and in workers' compensation cases to find-out if you should receive Second Injury Fund benefits.

· Denied claim- If your injury claim has been denied then you will need an attorney if you want to pursue the matter further.

How Do I Find a Qualified Personal Injury or Workers' Compensation Attorney?

Choosing an attorney to represent you is a very important task but can be quite confusing given the numerous choices. Your decision should not be made based on advertising alone. The Internet and Yellow Pages are filled with attorney advertisements that all basically say the same thing. You should not hire an attorney solely based upon their Google Ad, commercial that they run or other advertising. You should not even hire us until you are convinced that we are the right attorneys for your case.

How Do You Choose?

How do you find out which attorney is the best for your case? We believe that there are certain questions you should ask that will lead you to the best attorney for your case no matter what type of claim that you have. It will involve you spending some time and reading some materials, but choosing the right attorney is an important decision.

Personal injury, accident and workers' compensation cases are far too specialized for someone who does not regularly practice in these areas. Too often, we have looked at cases that inexperienced attorneys handled. The insurance companies keep track of and know which attorneys actually go to court and try cases and those who just settle. The insurance companies use this information to evaluate their risk. One of the first questions many insurance adjusters will ask when presented with a serious case is: Who represents the plaintiff? **If this is important to the insurance company, should it not also be important to you?** If you are represented by an attorney who does not have extensive experience going to court before a jury and trying serious injury cases or who "handles" a lot of injury cases but settles them all, then your case may be at risk.

So, How do You Find Out Who is Good in Your Area? Here Are Some Tips

1. The Internet. Google reviews are statements made by prior client. Also, websites like www.Avvo.com are independent, rate attorneys on a scale of 1 to 10 and allow clients and other attorneys to post comments about the attorney. Before you decide to talk to the attorney you

have been referred to or you found online check out www.Avvo.com.

2. Get a referral from an attorney that you know. He or she may know someone who does specializes in the area of law that you need. If you don't know anyone at all, then you can use the internet and yellow pages to find names and information.

3. However, **make sure to ask each attorney if they have information just like this book,** a DVD and/or a web site so that you can find out more about qualifications, experience, results, and verdicts, what past clients have to say and how they plan to handle your case before you walk in the door.

4. Television and the Yellow Pages. You should understand three things about TV commercials and the Yellow Pages: First, nowadays many attorneys advertise on TV and not as many advertise in the Yellow Pages. For example, many of our cases come from referrals from other attorneys and from satisfied clients. Second, be careful about the ads from a single attorney who touts too many different specialties (for example family law, criminal law, personal injury, workers' compensation), no one can do everything well. Third, be careful because this advertising typically attracts a lot of cases, including the small cases that we do not accept. Make sure that the attorney you hire is selective enough with his or her cases that your important case does not become just one more file in the pile.

5. The Iowa State Bar Association does have an attorney referral service. However, please understand that attorneys have signed up and paid a fee to be listed in certain specialties. Their names come up on a rotating basis. This

is another good source for an initial appointment. Just take the questions we talk about here to that interview.

6. Ask your attorney if he or she is licensed in the state where your case will be filed. We believe that an attorney who is not licensed in the state where the case will be filed is at a disadvantage when it comes to negotiating with the insurance company. The insurance companies know who is not licensed and thus cannot actually try the case. We recently came across a tragic story involving an out-of-state attorney who evaluated an Iowa car accident case. This attorney kept the file for almost two years and gave it back to the client just one week prior to the expiration of the statute of limitations. The problem was that the attorney told the client that he had another year to file the case, but this was based on the statute of limitations in his own state. The client was then prohibited from pursuing his case in Iowa.

7. Be careful about any attorney who rushes you to sign a contingent fee agreement. A contingent fee is not the right fee for every type of injury case. We know of cases in which attorneys have taken large fees on cases in which they did very little to deserve the fee. In fact, some attorneys have lost their license to practice law for engaging in these practices. Also, beware of an attorney who immediately wants to send you to one of his or her doctors.

8. Here are factors and good points to look for and question your attorney about. Note that not every attorney will meet all these criteria, but the significant absence of the following should be a big question mark.

• **Google Reviews-** This is where many people start and is a good indicator of how well they treat their clients, but it should not be the only factor.

• **Client Satisfaction-** Ask the attorney to show you what their past clients have to say about their legal services. They should have a booklet of testimonials and/or videos from prior clients.

• **Attorney Rating-** Does the attorney have a rating of "superb" on the attorney rating site www.Avvo.com? This rating involves a combination of what the attorney has written; education; experience; what other attorneys and clients have said about the attorney; and various other factors.

• **Experience actually trying cases** — Ask the attorney how many cases they have actually tried before a judge or jury. What is their track record? Have they achieved any significant verdicts or settlements? Does the attorney have a list of verdicts and settlements available that you can look at? Don't accept the "All my cases are confidential" line! The greater number of cases actually tried with substantial verdicts and settlements achieved, the more likely the insurance companies will respect the attorney. Past results are not a guarantee of the future, but past results do demonstrate some level of experience and success. Also, what do their past clients have to say?

• **Respect in the legal community-** Does the attorney teach other attorneys in Continuing Legal Education courses?

• **Membership and role in Associations-** In your area, you can certainly find attorneys who are members of the Iowa Association for Justice and the American Association for Justice, formerly known as the Association of Trial Lawyers of America (ATLA). All of these organizations provide extensive education and networking for trial lawyers.

• **Publications-** Has the attorney written anything that has been accepted for publication? This is another sign of respect that the legal community has for his or her skills and experience.

Once You Have Decided on an Attorney, Make Sure You Both Understand Your Goals and You Understand How the Relationship Will Work

1. How will your attorney keep you informed about the progress of the case? In our practice, we usually send a copy of every letter and pleading in the case to the client. We also take time to explain the "pace" of the case and in what time frames the client can expect activity to take place. Our clients are invited to call or email us at anytime. We will usually call or email you within 24 hours, unless our time is being devoted to a trial. Also, our assistants can schedule a "telephone appointment." Finally, you are invited to make an appointment to come in at a time that is convenient to you.

2. Find out who will actually be working on your case. Make sure that you and your attorney understand who your case will be assigned to. There are a lot of things that go

on in a case that do not require an experienced trial attorney's attention. On the other hand, if you are hiring an attorney because of his or her trial skills, make sure that the attorney you hired is going to be trying your case for you.

If you decide that we are not the firm for you, we recommend that you contact one or more of the following attorneys listed in alphabetical order:

Personal Injury (Car, Motorcycle and Truck Accidents, Dog Bites)

Tom Drew- Des Moines, Iowa- (515)-323-5640

Fred James- Des Moines, Iowa- (515)-246-8484

R. Saffin Parrish-Sams Des Moines- (515) 222-1697

Workers' Compensation

Jason Neifert- Des Moines- (515)-226-2117

Tom Palmer- (515) 223-8860

R. Saffin Parrish-Sams Des Moines- (515) 222-1697

Write any questions, comments, or concerns that you may have in the space below:

Page left blank intentionally.

Chapter 15

What Do We Do for You if You Hire Us?

Here is a list of the tasks we most likely will do in your case. Please keep in mind that each case is different, and that not all of these tasks will be required in every case. They are:

- Initial interview with the client
- Educate our client about the personal injury and workers' compensation laws
- Gather documentary evidence including police accident reports, medical records, and bills
- Hire an investigator, if necessary, to interview witnesses, locate witnesses, etc.
- Collect other evidence, such as photographs of the vehicles and accident scene
- Review and analyze the client's health insurance policy or other benefits plan to ascertain whether any money they spent to pay your bills must be repaid
- Analyze the client's insurance policy to see whether there are any coverages which the client has that may pay all or a portion of the medical bills while the claim is pending

- Analyze the client's insurance coverages and make suggestions as to what coverages should be purchased for future protection

- Review and analyze the legal issues, such as comparative fault and assumption of the risk

- Talk to the client's physicians or obtain written reports from them to fully understand the client's condition

- Review and analyze the validity of any liens on the case. Doctors, insurance companies, welfare benefit plans and employers may assert that they are entitled to all or part of the client's recovery

- Contact the insurance company to put them on notice of the claim, if this has not already been done

- Decide with the client whether an attempt will be made to negotiate the case with the insurance company or whether suit shall be filed

- If suit is filed, prepare the client, witnesses and healthcare providers for depositions

- Prepare written questions and answers and take the deposition of the defendant and other witnesses

- Produce to the defendant all of the pertinent data for the claim, such as medical bills, medical records, and tax returns

- Conduct a scheduling conference to set a trial date

- Prepare a demand package to send to the defendant in attempt to settle the case

- Prepare for a possible mediation and/or settlement before trial

- Prepare for trial

- Organize the preparation of medical exhibits for trial

- Organize the preparation of demonstrative exhibits for trial

- Prepare the client and witnesses for trial

- File motions with the court to determine what will be allowed into evidence at trial

- Take the case to trial with a jury in most personal injury cases or to a judge in workers' compensation cases

- Review and analyze the verdict to determine if either side has good grounds to appeal the case

- Make recommendations to the client as to whether or not to appeal the case

The Legal Process in Personal Injury and Workers' Compensation Cases

In many cases today, attempting to negotiate with the insurance company before filing suit is not worth the effort. Insurance companies often use the pre-suit negotiation only to attempt to find out as much about you, your lawyer and your doctor as they can. Many lawyers waste precious time attempting to negotiate with the insurance company before filing suit. If we accept your case, it is because we believe that it has legal merit and that you deserve a trial if we are not able to reach a settlement. Often, we will file your suit before negotiating so that if negotiations break down, we will already have a trial date in place to head towards.

It is a dangerous practice to wait until the last minute before the statute of limitations expires to file suit. We have seen other attorneys do this only to find that the defendant they sued is either not the correct defendant or is now blaming someone else which can ruin the case.

While there can be legitimate reasons for waiting to file suit, there is no excuse for the practice that some attorneys use when they routinely wait until the last minute in hopes that the insurance company will settle your case. Unfortunately, we have also seen lawyers not licensed in Iowa attempt to represent people with claims in those jurisdictions. When the claims do not settle, they often panic to find an attorney to file the case on time. (We have received plenty of those last-minute calls for help, and we reject them because inaction is not going to be our crisis.). It is a dangerous practice for a client to hire an attorney who is not licensed in the jurisdiction where suit must be filed.

Once the lawsuit is filed, both sides engage in what is called discovery. Discovery is the process in which both sides "discover" what the evidence will be and what the other side will present at trial. The defendant will be permitted access to your medical records, work records and income tax returns. You may be required to give a deposition under oath and be required to submit to a medical examination by a doctor hired by the defendant. We are also allowed to conduct discovery upon the defendant. The defendant will have to answer written questions called interrogatories, produce documents and be required to answer questions under oath in a deposition.

Write any questions, comments, or concerns that you may have in the space below:

Page left blank intentionally.

Chapter 16

How Can This Be Happening to Me? Stories of Survival

Take for example, Rod, one of our clients. Rod is a hard-working father of two who was driving home from work. As he went through a green light, he was hit in the driver's door by a drunk driver who ran the red light. Not only was the driver drunk, but he did not have insurance and had been drinking at a local bar. Rod sustained serious injuries requiring him to have several surgeries, and he was off work for almost 1 year. Thankfully, for Rod, he had read Corey's car insurance book and had bought enough insurance coverage to protect him and his family. Also, it was good that he went to see Corey shortly after the crash.

Corey was able to find out where the drunk driver had been drinking and send the bar a Dramshop notice within the 6-month deadline.

While Rod will live with daily pain and some permanent problems, he now has the financial security that he deserves for going through such a terrible crash. Also, the bar that over served the driver has changed its policies and procedures so hopefully another family will not have to go through what Rod and his family have.

You Can't Believe How Some Insurance Companies Try To Rip People Off...

Jan was involved in what the insurance company called a "minor" fender bender, when her car was struck in the rear. The damage to her vehicle was about $2,000, but her car was drivable. Because she did not have immediate pain, she did not go to the hospital. When she woke-up the next day she was very sore and had a headache, so she went to see her family doctor. Her doctor said that she should get better with physical therapy, but after a few months she was not getting better. Her doctor referred her for testing, which found that she had suffered a serious spinal injury.

She was sent to a specialist for an operation to repair her neck. The operation cost thousands of dollars and Jan could not work for several months while she was recovering. Even with the surgery, **Jan's neck will never be the same.**

Since she did not go to the hospital immediately after the accident, she did not know if she would be able to make a claim for the pain and disability she was now experiencing. The insurance company told her that they would only pay a small portion of her medical bills, plus a few hundred dollars for her pain and suffering injuries. The insurance company went by the damage of her car, which was minimal at the time of the accident, yet Jan had suffered two herniated discs in her neck. Understandably, Jan began asking questions like:

· Do I have the right to be compensated for more than what the insurance company is offering me?

· Do I need to see an attorney?

· How do I choose a good attorney who has experience?

Jan was seriously injured, scared, and very confused. When Jan came to see us, she was at her wit's end, ready to sign her rights away so she could at least get "something." The insurance company refused to accept that she was seriously injured from a so-called "low impact" injury. **Many "low impact" accidents do cause hidden injuries if the occupant is not expecting a sudden impact, like Jan.**

Fortunately for Jan, she came to see us before signing her rights away to the insurance company or hiring an inexperienced attorney. She could have easily taken this quick (and inadequate) settlement. We were able to take the pressure off Jan while we took the insurance company to court to force them to live up to their legal **"obligations."** Most importantly, we sat down with Jan and explained what her rights were concerning the personal injuries she had suffered. She never understood what was involved with the legal process until we told her that she had "rights," including compensation for the pain and suffering she was experiencing from this accident. We gathered Jan's medical records together and over a period of several months of negotiations was able to obtain a fair and just settlement. It took some time, but it was acceptable to Jan and us. The bottom line is that the settlement was "right", and it was what Jan deserved.

Work Injuries- How Will I Make It? John's Story

My name is John and I live in a small town in northern Iowa with my wife and young son in a house that we recently purchased. Our families live nearby, and our life was good until one day at work in 2015, I developed back pain while lifting at work in a local factory. I reported my work injury to my employer and asked for medical care. At first, I did not think it was a big deal, but little did I know how my life would be changed forever. The pain in my back and then down into my legs got worse and the testing revealed that I had a herniated disc in my back. After waiting what seemed like forever for medical care, eventually I was allowed to see a back surgeon who thought that surgery consisting of a laminectomy/diskectomy on my lower back would fix my problems.

My first back surgery did not help, so a 2nd more invasive surgery called a lumbar fusion was recommended. Once again, the surgery provided little pain relief so a 3rd procedure consisting of putting a permanent spinal cord stimulator was recommended. The stimulator provides some pain relief, but both physically and mentally I will never be the same person again. Before my injury, I was physically fit and able to help family and friends with construction projects, play in a local softball league and volunteer at our church. Now, I cannot even physically play with my son and have to use a cane to walk outside of my home. I do not sleep very well and often have to sleep in my recliner. When I see my wife in the morning, I often ask her "how can I go on like this."

While I was off work healing after my fusion surgery it was clear to my wife and I that I was not going to be able to return to my same manual labor job. I thought that because I was hurt at work, my employer had to provide me with a job. When I was told that my lifting restrictions were permanent, after missing more than 1 year of work because of my injury, my employer decided that they would not bring me back to work. I was unemployed, scared and confused about the future of me and my family. We were behind on some of our bills and wanted to avoid losing everything we had worked so hard for. We just wanted to be treated fairly by the insurance company, but we did not understand what that meant under the Iowa workers' compensation laws.

Given that we were facing a financial disaster we decided that we better find an attorney to help us through the work comp. process. We did not have the money to pay an attorney an hourly fee and I was worried that hiring an attorney may look bad to my friends, my employer and the insurance company. We were barely making it with the weekly check I was receiving so we could not afford to pay an attorney up front. Also, I had never dealt with an attorney before so I was afraid about contacting one and how I may be treated. However, I knew that given I had been fired, my employer and their insurance company were not looking out for my best interests, and I needed someone to help protect me.

I began looking online and wanted to find an attorney who was not only good at what he does, but also took care of his clients and treated them right. I found Iowa attorney Corey Walker who had dozens of positive reviews and videos from prior clients. He was not local to me, but I went ahead and called him even though I had doubts if he could help me or not. He sent me a copy of his Iowa workers' compensation book and DVD at no cost. Corey's book and other information opened my eyes revealing many things I did not know about work comp. here in Iowa.

When I called Corey with questions, to my surprise he agreed to travel 3 hours to my home to meet with my wife and a few of my family members at no cost or risk. I did not know what to expect at our meeting with Corey. When he walked into our home, I immediately felt comfortable with him as he took his time to explain how the system works and was very patient with the many questions that we had. He explained that I did not have to pay him a retainer and he only was paid if he obtained more money than the insurance company voluntarily paid me so what did I have to lose? He was not like attorneys on TV as he did not try to pressure me or scare me into hiring him. There was no up-front cost or risk to me so given all the prior great client reviews I was sure that he was the best attorney to help me and my family, but I still wondered if I did the right thing by hiring Corey.

Corey requested my wage records and within 2 months he found that I was being underpaid by more than $35 per week. He was able to get me a check for the money they underpaid, plus interest and a new higher weekly check. Then he filed a workers' compensation petition on my behalf seeking benefits for the rest of my life. Also, when the insurance company did not want to pay for the treatment that their own doctors recommended, he helped obtain the medical care by filing a petition for alternative medical care. Every step of the way Corey was committed to helping me. He sent copies of letters, returned my phone calls, and took his time to explain what and why he was doing things. I could not have asked for a better attorney to fight for my rights and help me through the process. As our trial date quickly approached, Corey explained the different possible outcomes and sent a demand to the insurance company's lawyer in an attempt to settle the case and avoid years of appeals. He spent many hours working on the demand letter and helping us understand what was best for me and my family.

He kept us informed at each step of the negotiation process and after several weeks of negotiating just prior to my trial, he was able to obtain a lump-sum of money that allowed us to pay off our home loan and purchase a reliable vehicle while still having money in the bank for our future. While I would never trade my health for the money that I received, with Corey's hard work at least I have a secure financial future. I cannot recommend him enough to other Iowans dealing with a serious work injury.

How Will I Get Back to Work?

Take for example, Karen, one of our clients. Karen was a 35 year old wife and mother of three working in the factory. Karen was a dependable worker who always came to work on time and had not missed a day of work in 4 years. Unfortunately, Karen was lifting a heavy part at work when her back gave-out. She ended up on the floor in severe pain. Karen immediately went to medical and reported that she had hurt her back at work. The medical personnel told her to go see her family doctor and return to work with what he says. Karen's family doctor prescribed pain medications and excused her from work for the next week. However, Karen's condition worsened and after only two days she was back seeing her family doctor. Her doctor ordered an MRI, which confirmed that Karen had suffered a herniated disc in her back. Karen was referred on to a surgeon for evaluation of the herniated disc. The surgeon told her that surgery was her best option as the disc would likely not heal on its own. Karen was devastated because she had never had surgery before and had always taken pride in her work.

While Karen had the surgery and made a good recovery, the doctor assigned her a 10% impairment rating and placed a permanent 30-pound lifting restriction upon her. She was not able to return to her higher paying line job, but had to take a lower paying job. She was satisfied with the 50 weeks of benefits they paid her but did not realize that she was entitled to much more compensation for her injuries.

Thankfully for Karen, one of her friends had previously been injured at his job and we handled his case for him.

Karen came to see us and we informed her that her case was worth much more than the 50 weeks of benefits she had been paid. She was entitled to industrial disability in which her impairment rating was only one of many factors. Karen eventually settled her case for more than twice as much as the insurance company had previously paid her. If Karen had not come to see us, she would have missed out on more than $50,000 in money owed to her.

Jim's Struggle with An Insurance Company Denial

Another client, Jim, was a hard-working truck driver and father of two children. While he was driving his employer's tractor-trailer, he was involved in an accident causing him to sustain two broken bones in his back. He was immediately transported to the nearest trauma center where he spent the next several days. Doctors told Jim that he was lucky that he was not paralyzed and a few days later he was released from the hospital and told to follow-up with his family doctor.

Jim notified his employer of the accident and the insurance company called him to take a statement. Jim told the insurance adjustor exactly what happened and a few days later he received a letter stating that they were denying his claim and not paying his lost wages or medical expenses. Jim was desperate when he came to our office as he was not receiving any income. We did some checking up. We obtained the accident report, hired a private investigator and contacted the insurance company about their previous decision. Once we intervened in the case, the insurance company decided that Jim's claim was legitimate and began paying him for his lost wages. After missing several months of work, Jim made a satisfactory recovery and we were able to obtain a "just" settlement for him.

This Next Case We See Way Too Often.

Another client, Mike was a 25-year-old living his dream. Mike's dream was to save enough money to buy an older home and then to remodel it. Mike had always loved working with his hands and building things. After high school, Mike worked full-time at a factory making good money.

Mike's dream turned into a nightmare when he was involved in a roll-over crash while riding with a friend. His friend lost control of his car causing the vehicle to go into the ditch and roll. Because Mike sustained a brain injury and broken bones he was taken by helicopter to the hospital. Surgeons were able to save his life with emergency surgery. After spending 2 weeks in the hospital, he was transferred to a rehabilitation facility for him to relearn how to walk and do other activities of daily living.

Mike was no longer able to work, and his family was desperate to get him help. Mike and his family hired a lawyer that they knew from around town who did divorces, wills and criminal defense. Months went by with no results. Mike's lawyer could not answer many of his questions because he did not specialize in personal injury law. Would you let your general practice family doctor perform surgery to remove your appendix? Then why would you let a general practice attorney handle your personal injury case? You need someone who practices primarily in personal injury law.

Mike was falling seriously behind on his bills and his dream of owning a home was almost gone. Through no fault of his own, Mike was now facing financial ruin. Mike and his family were understandably distraught when they called our office. We got right on his case and our investigation revealed that his friend was driving a vehicle owned by his father who had an umbrella policy to cover his damages.

We made a claim for Mike against the driver and owner of the vehicle he was riding in. Mike's friend attempted to avoid responsibility by blaming road conditions and attacking Mike, the **innocent victim.** The Defendants said, "Mike was exaggerating his brain injury." Well, we filed suit for Mike and made the Defendants answer to Mike and his family in court. Mike's medical expenses, lost income and loss of enjoyment of life were significant. He was no longer the same ambitious, caring, and loving person as he was before the accident. The jury accepted our contentions and returned a substantial verdict to Mike that included payment of his past and future medical bills, lost income, permanent injuries, and pain and suffering <u>for the rest of his life.</u>

The best news for Mike was that the jury verdict allowed him to purchase his own home and hire workers to do the needed renovation work he can no longer do. While Mike will never be the same, he is at least **living part of his dream.** While your case may not be as serious as Mike's you still deserve to be justly compensated.

Write any questions, comments, or concerns that you may have in the space below:

Page left blank intentionally.

Chapter 17

14 MYTHS ABOUT IOWA CAR ACCIDENT, WORK INJURY AND PERSONAL INJURY CASES

- If you are reasonable with the insurance company, then they will be reasonable with you.

- The insurance adjustor is there to help you with your injury case.

- If you have a medical case manager assigned to your case, you have to let them in the examination room during your exam.

- If your doctor says to return as needed you do not need to return even if you continue to have pain and medical problems.

- Attorneys who run television commercials must be good.

- All attorneys who advertise that they handle car accident, personal injury and/or workers' compensation cases have the same skills, education, tools, and experience to handle your case.

- All attorneys charge the same fees.

- All attorneys are personally involved in the cases they handle.

- When you are in an accident and the insurance company asks for a recorded statement, you have to give it to them, or they won't settle with you.

- In a workers' compensation case you can sue your employer for negligence.

- In a workers' compensation case you can recover for your pain and suffering.

- In car accident and personal injury cases the insurance company for the other party is obligated to pay your medical bills and lost wages as they are incurred.

- In car accident and personal injury cases just because there has been an accident and it wasn't your fault, the insurance company for the other party will treat you fairly.

- In car accident and personal injury cases juries in Iowa are generous.

Chapter 18

Why Should You Consider Hiring Us?

As we said at the beginning of this book, "we are not your average Iowa attorneys." Instead of running around trying to manage hundreds of cases at a time, we carefully select the few cases that we will accept at any one time.

There are many attorneys who advertise for personal injury cases. Unfortunately, some of these attorneys have so many small cases in their offices that no case gets their personal attention. Others have no real intention of trying your case themselves and if the case cannot be settled with the insurance company, they will refer the case out for trial. Many will not even bother to talk with your doctors until they ask for their opinions for the first time during a deposition. There are good, experienced attorneys in this field, but it can be very difficult for a consumer to separate the good from the bad.

PERSONAL ATTENTION

Our clients get personal attention because we are very selective in the cases that we take. We decline dozens of cases each year so we can devote personal, careful attention to those clients that we accept. We take the time and spend the money to go meet with your doctors and explain to them how they can assist in your case. We prepare every case like it is going to trial because we do not know which ones will need to be tried until the end. We also follow the **Golden Rule** and treat our clients like we want to be treated which means we return phone calls, respond to emails, answer your questions, explain the legal process, send you copies of letters and generally keep you informed about your case. Also, we offer our unique Injured Iowans First Recovery Agreement™.

To better serve our clients we have fully staffed offices located in Ankeny, Des Moines/Urbandale, Marshalltown, and Newton along with by appointment only locations throughout Iowa, including Cedar Rapids, Waterloo, Davenport, Dubuque, Decorah, Grinnell, Ottumwa, Council Bluffs, and Sioux City. If you are not local to one of our offices, then we can come to you. Also, homebound appointments are available.

What Cases Do We Generally Not Accept?

Due to the very high volume of calls and referrals from other attorneys that we receive, we have found that the only way to provide personal service is to decline those cases that do not meet our strict criteria. Therefore, we generally do not accept the following types of cases:

□ Car accident cases involving little or no damage to the vehicles, generally defined as having less than $500 in property damage to your car. Our experience with juries is that by and large, they do not believe that minor impacts can cause substantial personal injury. We have tried several cases where we felt that the medical evidence was very strong, yet the photographs and the property damage showed little or no damage. Even though we had well-qualified physicians who testified that our clients were injured in the accident, these cases were either lost or resulted in very low verdicts. Therefore, we believe the risk and time spent by the client are too great and that our time is better spent helping those with other cases. There are other attorneys with different opinions about these cases

and, again, we will be happy to supply you with several names.

☐ If you are done treating and you have less than $5,000 of total "hard damages." Your case must have at least $5,000 in total past and future medical bills and/or past and future lost wages before we will consider accepting it. Please keep in mind this is not just out of pocket expenses such as co-pays and deductibles, these include the "total" medical charges. We would like to represent everyone who needs a good attorney, but we cannot because just like everyone else we only have 24 hours in a day and enjoy spending time with our loved ones. If you have a question about this, contact us and we can help you figure it out.

☐ Cases with significant pre-existing injury in the same body part. For example, if you were treating with a doctor for a back injury at the time of your accident and continue to have back problems after the accident, then the chances of a jury awarding you a substantial amount of money for your back injuries is reduced. Again, we feel that it is not worth taking the time from our other clients to pursue these cases.

☐ We will not represent you if you were found at fault and charged by the police in the accident. We know that the police can be wrong; but if after interviewing the witnesses and evaluating the scene, the officer gave you a ticket and not the other person, then we will not represent you.

Workers' Compensation

□ Cases in which you make a full recovery and no longer have any problems. Likewise, if the doctor says that you have no permanent impairment rating or no permanent restrictions and you are able to go back to your same job making the same money. While you may be owed more than what the insurance company pays you in these cases, we believe that our time is better spent helping those with permanent injuries that affect their ability to work. However, if you wonder if we will take your case, please call us and we will let you know. If we do not take your case then we will refer you to someone who may.

ALL INJURY CASES

□ Cases where the statute of limitations will soon run out. we like to have at least 3 months to adequately investigate and evaluate your claim. Your delay is not going to become our crisis- taking away from our other clients. Note: in workers' compensation cases your statute of limitations may be extended past the standard 2 years if you have received weekly workers' compensation checks.

□ If your case has already been filed, we will not represent you. We like to do things our way. If you or another attorney has already filed the case, that's fine, but we will not handle the matter.

There are attorneys who do mass advertising and accept small cases so if we do not accept your case we will be happy to refer you to several such attorneys.

Well, Are There Any Cases Left?

Yes, there are, and that is the point because with hard work and personal attention we **Level the Field Between Injured Iowans and Insurance Companies™ by Fighting for Justice and Respect.™**

"We Concentrate our Efforts on Increasing the Value of the Good Cases—Not Filing and Pursuing Smaller Ones"

We represent many clients with significant valid claims. When we devote our time and resources to representing only legitimate claimants with good claims, we are able to do our best work. We have found that spending countless hours on lots of little cases, each with a "unique problem," is not good for our other clients.

Write any questions, comments, or concerns that you may have in the space below:

Page left blank intentionally.

Chapter 19

What Do Our Past Clients Have to Say?

We represented hundreds of clients, and the vast majority of them have been happy with our legal services. Remember that each case is different and past results are not a guarantee that you will be happy with our services. With this being said, here is what some of our past clients have to say. In order to preserve confidentiality, only their first names and location are listed. If you would like to **watch what our clients say about us** go to www.OurClientsTalk.com.

Car Accidents and Personal Injury

Corey is the best and most professional lawyer I have ever known. He represented me far and above any expectations I had. He went to bat for me hit a double Grand Slam. He respects his clients and puts their needs above anything else. I know that he is very trustworthy and professional. I would, have and will continue to recommend him. Again, Corey Walker is the best. Thank you for representing me, Corey.

Don of Des Moines, Iowa (Salesperson)

I have had to use lawyers in the past. None have done the work or explained things like this law firm. Thanks all of you.

James of Smithland (Construction worker)

I sustained permanent brain injuries in a motor vehicle accident in which liability was disputed. Attorney Corey J. L. Walker took the time to thoroughly prepare the case for trial, hire the experts that we needed and listen to me and my family. While I will never be the same person as I was before the accident, I now have financial security. I recommend that if you have sustained injuries that you talk to them to see if you may be able to recover for your injuries.

Jeff of Pella, Iowa (former factory worker, now disabled)

My daughter was seriously injured in a car accident when she was a passenger in a car without insurance. The driver of the car lost control causing a serious crash. I made a claim against my insurance company for uninsured motorists' benefits, but they refused to pay. I scheduled an appointment with Corey to going over our rights and to find out what we could do. Corey was very helpful and was able to obtain the most money possible under our insurance policy. Unfortunately, I had not bought enough insurance to cover all of my daughter's injuries caused in the crash. If you or a loved one have been injured by a driver without insurance, you should contact Corey to learn about your rights. He will look out for your best interests and make sure the insurance company pays what they owe.

Alicia of Des Moines, Iowa (Office worker)

I was riding in a friend's car when we were hit by a driver who ran a red light. I was wearing my seat belt, but still suffered injuries to my neck, back and arm. I had to go to physical therapy and about a month after the accident discovered I also had a serious injury to my leg. I was hospitalized and missed over one month of work. Erik met with my doctors and convinced the insurance companies that my leg injury was caused by the car accident. Unfortunately, the driver who ran the red light did not have enough so Erik went after my underinsured motorist coverage through my own insurance company. They did not want to pay so we took them to court and eventually they settled for my policy limits. Erik was very helpful and was able to obtain the most money possible from all the insurance policies involved.

Jenny of Des Moines, Iowa (Student)

When I was injured by a person who drank too much at a bar, I called Corey to find out what I needed to do. It is a good thing that I called him because I only had 6 months to file a notice with the bar to pursue a dramshop claim. If you are injured by someone who was drunk you should call Corey right away to protect your rights.

Rob of Newton, Iowa (Salesperson)

I sustained a serious injury in a motorcycle crash in which the insurance company was disputing who was at fault for the accident and initially offered me very little to settle my case. Corey J. L. Walker took the time to thoroughly prepare the case for trial and obtain the medical opinions we needed. As a result of his professionalism and preparation we obtained a good settlement. I recommend that if you have sustained injuries in an automobile accident that you go talk to Corey and not just take what the insurance company is offering you.

Duane of Marion County (Realtor)

I was injured and the insurance company denied that the other driver was at fault, so I called attorney Corey J. L. Walker. Corey filed suit, worked hard and fought to obtain a $190,000 settlement for me. While my leg will never be the same, at least I will have some financial security to get back on my feet. If you have been injured then you should go see Corey because he will hold the wrongdoer accountable.

John of Indianola, Iowa (Construction worker)

Attorney Erik Bair handled my son's case when he was injured at school while students were allowed to work in the auto shop over the lunch hour without any supervision. My son was injured when he was picked up and thrown to the ground by an older student. We obtained a good settlement with the school district because of Erik's hard work and dedication. Erik kept us informed with everything that was going on with the case and quickly returned our phone calls. We are pleased with Erik's services and would recommend Erik to anyone.

Jessica of Jefferson, Iowa (Teacher)

We had a great experience with Erik. I highly encourage you to use this firm, specifically Erik. Erik communicated with us throughout the process, returned phone calls/emails promptly and called to just update us on the case. He went above and beyond to get what we deserved. We are extremely happy. The service provided was beyond great.

Dillon Romanco of Pleasantville, Iowa (service worker)

I sustained an injury in a motor vehicle accident involving a UPS truck. Their insurance company claimed that I was partially at fault for the accident and refused to pay for the damage to my car. I called attorney Corey J. L. Walker and he took the time to talk to me about my case and explain my rights. He filed a lawsuit for me and because of his hard work we were able to obtain a just settlement. I recommend that if you have sustained injuries in an automobile accident and the insurance company is not playing by the rules that you go talk to Corey because he will fight for you.

Cindy of Des Moines, Iowa (Secretary)

Attorney Corey J. L. Walker handled a wrongful death case for me when my son was killed in an automobile accident. We pursued the property owner who had failed to install a barricade which resulted in the vehicle my son was riding in to leave the roadway causing his death. He handled the case in a professional, aggressive and efficient matter. Corey helped me in obtaining a substantial settlement against the negligent property owner.

Melissa of Newton, Iowa (Production worker)

When I was injured in a car accident by a driver without insurance I contacted Walker & Billingsley for help. Attorney Corey Walker explained to me that because the other driver did not have insurance that I would need to make a claim against my own insurance company. At first, my insurance company did not want to pay for my injuries, but with Corey's guidance and hard work we were able to reach a fair settlement. He kept me informed about my case and was even able to negotiate a reduced payment with my health insurance company to put more money in my pocket. If you have been injured in a car accident, then I recommend that you go see Corey.

Jennifer of Kellogg, Iowa (Bookkeeper)

Thank you very much for helping me get through this claim and being a listening post, I couldn't have done it without your help. I appreciated your kindness and help, again I thank you.

Sheila of Pleasantville, Iowa (Store clerk)

A careless driver was going too fast and lost control of his car and crashed into me. My car was totaled and I had to have multiple surgeries because of the crash. I hired Erik to help me and he did an outstanding job. His office and staff are great and I will recommend them to anyone I know who has been hurt in a car accident.

Daren of Polk County, Iowa (Factory worker)

Highly recommend! Professional, trustworthy, friendly, knowledgeable and caring. Answers all questions and concerns in a timely fashion. Keeps you updated at all times. Their services were excellent! Above and beyond and more than I hoped for.

Shan of Clinton, Iowa (Medical Tech)

Corey is an outstanding attorney. He made me feel likely I was his only client and I know others had more pressing issues. He treated me like I was important. Corey will do his best and make it easy and understandable. He will be honest and will do things in a timely manner. He will not make you feel dumb. I think you guys do a great job!!

Kris of Eldora (Service Provider)

Workers' Compensation

I had never called an attorneys office before and now I'm very glad I did. Corey Walker and his staff treated me with respect from the very beginning. I felt very comfortable from the first time I talked to him. Corey showed me that there are still people who care about other people and fight for our rights. I would have never received a dime if it wasn't for Corey. I will recommend his law firm to anyone. Also, the secretaries were big help and very respectful to me. Thank you and once again, you have brought back my faith in the system.

Robin of Hardin County (Factory worker)

Mr. Bair was very helpful in my case and he was very respectful. He contacted me about concerns for my case and kept me updated. I would recommend Erik to all my friends or relatives that would be looking for an attorney. I've enjoyed reading the monthly newsletter I hope I can continue to receive one in the mail. I want to say thank you Mr. Bair you went out of your way to help me.

Rene of Madrid, Iowa (Farm worker)

This was my real first attorney experience. I was scared and uncomfortable. Joanie made all those feelings go away. She was wonderful to be around and work with. I would go to Joanie again. She truly cares and treats you like a human, not just another case. She did so much to help me, above and beyond what I expected.

Jeff of Marshalltown, Iowa (Factory worker)

I am very pleased with the service that I was given for my circumstance in the case with regard to injuries that I've sustained and physical current outcome. When it came to negotiating, Erik listened to me and was able to get me close to what I was trying to get so I could help secure my family's home without being stressed. I would say that you feel as if you're the only person that they are working for, due to the fact that they are quick to respond to phone calls and e-mails. Also they are very detailed in explaining every step of your case and are people you can trust. I'm very happy with the services that I received. Thanks for all that you and your team do for people like me.

Shawn of Ankeny (Maintenance)

I want to thank Attorney Grife for her hard and dedicated work on my behalf. I truly feel she went above and beyond the norm to win my litigation case. I also know she is a superb attorney, whom if needed I will recommend and call on again. My deepest gratitude goes out to her and her associates. It is nice to know you are represented by such a quality attorney. Thank you Mrs. Grife!

Rodney of Clinton, Iowa (Store clerk)

I was injured at a nursing job I had worked at for more than 20 years. Because of my injuries, I could not return to my previous job. I talked to several attorneys about handling my case, but then I met with Corey. He took the time to answer my questions and explain all the aspects of my case. I am glad I chose Corey because he was able to obtain a fair settlement in my case and now I can move on with my life.

Kathy of Marshalltown, Iowa (RN-registered nurse)

Totally satisfied with everything and how it was handled. I was referred to Corey by a coworker and a relative and it was the best decision I made. Thank you very much for your services.

Larry of New Sharon, Iowa (Electrical engineer)

From start to finish everything was handled perfectly. I couldn't be more happy. I received more than I expected. Joanie is a great attorney and works for a fantastic firm. Thanks to the entire staff at Walker, Billingsley & Bair! I will refer you to others in need of help! If I need any future legal help I will be contacting you guys. I'll stick with the law firm that has proven itself to me.

Larry of Eldora (Production worker)

Erik was great right from the start. He explained how the case would proceed and answered my questions. He made me feel at ease and throughout the three years, he was always quick to respond to emails and calls. A friendship grew out of this stressful, painful time in my life and I just want to say "thank you" from the bottom of my heart.

Mary of Urbandale (RN- registered nurse)

Joanie Grife was a sweet angel. I felt very comfortable and at ease with her. I would like to thank you and your staff for all your support and efforts on my behalf. I was very happy with the outcome of my case. I will give reference to Joanie Grife's office.

Mary of Harper, Iowa (CNA)

I was hurt on the job breaking bones in my leg. The insurance company started paying me benefits, but then stopped and would not return my phone calls. I went to see Corey who explained to me the Iowa Workers' Compensation laws. He pursued my case and the insurance company paid the benefits they owed, plus interest. If you are hurt at work and the insurance company stops your benefits you should call Corey.

Andrew of Newton, Iowa (Construction worker)

When I came to Corey, I did not even know I had a case against the Second Injury Fund of Iowa. I only thought I had a case against my employer and their insurance company. The Second Injury Fund did not want to pay what the case was worth, so went to trial. While it did take some time to receive compensation, once I did, the ruling was for much more than I had expected. I would strongly recommend that others use Corey as an attorney in their workers' compensation cases. You may have a Second Injury Fund case and not even know it. If I had not called Corey about my workers' compensation case, I would have lost out on more than $100,000.

Bill of Polk County, Iowa (Truck driver)

I sustained an injury and the insurance company offered to settle my case. I suspected that their offer was too low and when I went to see Corey Walker, I was right. Corey helped me with my case and quickly obtained me the settlement that I deserved.

Randy of Boone, Iowa (Factory worker)

I would encourage anyone to hire an attorney from Walker, Billingsley & Bair Law Firm. My experience with your firm was outstanding. I wouldn't change anything. My phone calls and emails were always returned in a timely manner. Whenever I called the office the staff was always nice and pleasant and assisted me with the questions I had.

Quinten of Williamsburg, Iowa (Factory worker)

I hurt my back while working construction which is all I have ever done. Because of my back injury, I could not go back to working construction and was left with filing for workers' compensation and Social Security disability. Corey was able to negotiate a settlement which allowed me to keep my monthly Social Security disability benefits and receive a lump-sum settlement for my work injury. If I had not hired Corey, I would have lost almost 50% of my monthly Social Security benefits because of the Social Security disability offset. Corey saved me thousands of dollars of lost benefits and obtained a good settlement for me. If you have been injured at work and are considering filing for Social Security disability you should go talk to Corey. With his experience and hard work he will protect you and your rights.

Butch of Tama, Iowa (Construction worker)

Corey, you are my saving hero. The settlement you obtained for me after my back injury is what has kept me from 'going under' financially. There are not enough words to adequately express my appreciation for your excellent work on my behalf.

Gwen of Scranton, IA (Registered Nurse)

I hurt my shoulder at work and because of my injury, I could no longer do many of the jobs that I had done in the past. The insurance company made me an offer to settle my case. I had no idea if the offer was fair or not so I went to see Corey for a free consultation and audit of my case. He told me that the offer was too low and he filed a petition for benefits. If the insurance company makes an offer in your workers' compensation case, you should go see Corey. I am glad I did because with his hard work I received $25,000 more than the insurance company offered me before hiring Corey.

Gregg of Newton, Iowa (Maintenance worker)

I hurt my neck while working for a local company. Even though I had to have neck surgery, my employer and their insurance company denied that my neck injury was caused by work. I saw an ad for a free book about work injuries so I called and got the book. After reading his book, I hoped that Corey would help me with my case. Corey agreed to meet with me at no charge. At our meeting, he agreed to help me. He got my medical records and then had a conference with my surgeon to prove that my neck injury was work related. While the insurance company would not admit that my injury was work related, with Corey's help I was able to get a good settlement. If the insurance company denies that your injury is work related you should give Corey a call. If I had not called Corey I would have given-up thousands of dollars.

John of Story County, Iowa (Sanitation worker)

I worked at a hospital and fell in the parking lot on some ice. In the fall I injured my back, but the doctors told me that there was no surgery to fix it. My back pain became so severe that I could no longer do my job which required a lot of sitting along with bending over and retrieving files. The insurance company refused to provide additional treatment for my back injury so I went to see Corey. Corey went to meet with my doctors and was able to prove to the insurance company that my back injury was caused by my fall at work. He got my medical treatment started again and then got me a good settlement through mediation. I appreciate his dedication and hard work on my case.

Cindy of Altoona, Iowa (Billing clerk)

When the workers' compensation insurance company stopped paying me benefits for my shoulder injury, I went to see attorney Corey Walker. He handled my workers' compensation case in a professional and aggressive manner. He timely returned my phone calls and kept me informed of what was going on with my case. While it did take some time, he made the insurance company accept responsibility for my work injury and pay me fair compensation. If you have been hurt at work and are not being treated fairly, go talk to Corey because he will fight hard for your rights.

Lindsay of Knoxville, Iowa (Ambulance personnel)

Erik was outstanding and patient, a very good person and I thank him a lot.

Robert of Des Moines, Iowa (School Custodian)

I hurt my back when I fell in the factory. I went through physical therapy, but I still had problems. While I was able to return to work and do my job, I was eventually fired by the company. Despite losing my job, the insurance company did not offer to pay me any permanent benefits so

I went to see Corey. Corey filed a workers' compensation petition for me and was able to get me a good settlement before the trial. If I had not gone to see Corey then I would not have received any money for my back injury. If you have been hurt at work and are still having problems then go see Corey.

Wane of Newton, Iowa (Factory worker)

I was injured on the job when I fell from a roof sustaining severe and permanent injuries. The insurance company stopped making workers' compensation payments which I suspected was not right. I requested some information from Corey which he sent to me right away. Then I went to see him and he explained to me that the insurance company should not have stopped my benefits. He contacted the insurance company right away and my weekly benefits started again. He then filed a claim on my behalf and we were able to settle the case. If the insurance company stops your benefits, then you should go see Corey because you may be entitled to additional compensation.

Don of Ft. Dodge, Iowa (Roofer)

I sustained a back injury while lifting at work and had to have several surgeries. Corey helped me all the way through the workers' compensation process and helped get me the medical care that I needed. He explained everything to me, answered all my questions and was always there to talk about what was going on. While I cannot go back to physical labor work, Corey was able to get me enough money to move on with my life.

Michelle of Des Moines (Delivery Driver)

I sustained back and neck injuries at work and my employer's insurance company had not paid me any permanent benefits. I went to see Corey to find-out if they owed me anything. It turns out that they did so Corey filed a petition for me and we won. The insurance company did not want to pay so they appealed the decision dragging my case out for several years. Corey did not give-up and fought them all the way. In the end it paid-off because he got me a settlement of more than $100,000.

Beth of Marshall County (Janitor)

I would highly recommend Erik. He was knowledgeable, answered all my questions, and returned all phone calls in a timely manner. Erik was honest and explained the entire process in words I could understand. Erik took care of all the needed work and explained in detail what I needed to do on my part. I never had any doubts that Erik had my best intention at heart.

Kelly of Marion County (Nurse)

When I was having problems communicating with the insurance adjustor I decided to consider hiring an attorney. I found Corey in a local newspaper advertisement and gave him a call. Corey and his staff were excellent throughout the process and if I know someone who needs help with a legal matter I will give them Corey's phone number.

Mike of Spirit Lake (Truck driver)

I was very happy how I was treated. I was very happy with the settlement.

Mark of Decorah, Iowa (Mechanic)

Corey represented me when I hurt my knee at work which required surgery. It affected the way that I walked which lead to back pain and problems. My wife and I were scared and confused about what could happen to our only source of income, my job. We decided to meet with Corey in his Cedar Rapids office and have been very happy with him and his staff ever since. Corey fought for me and my family throughout the trial and the appeal process winning for me every step of the way. Without Corey's help I do not know where I would be right now. During the past several years that he has represented me Corey has become much more than my attorney, he has also become my friend. I highly recommend Corey and his team to anyone who has been injured in Iowa.

Arron of Cedar Rapids (Warehouse worker)

Joanie was an amazing attorney! She always talked me through every detail of my case so I always understood what was going on. She always returned my phone calls very quickly. I would've never gotten a settlement at all if it weren't for Joanie. My placement of employment tried making me feel I was in the wrong, and that I had no case. Joanie helped me see that I did have a very good case.

Angela of Dubuque, Iowa (C.N.A.)

I was extremely pleased with Joanie! I truly wish to thank her for all of her hard work. Thank you. Thank you.

Deb, Blue Grass, Iowa (Clinic office secretary)

For a listing of more of "What our Past Clients Have to Say" go to our Webpage at www.IowaInjured.com

Our Services

We are here to provide you with personal service and protect your rights throughout your case. Sometimes the best advice we can give is that you do not have a claim that can be won. If that is true, we will tell you so. If your case meets our criteria and we decide to accept your case, you will receive our personal attention. We provide you with copies of letters written and let you know what the current status is of your case. We will give you our advice as to whether your case should be settled or if we should proceed to trial where one or more of us will be the ones trying your case. Also, if you ever have any questions please feel free to contact one of us. We would rather have you call and ask your question rather than sit and wonder what the answer is. We are committed to providing the attention to details and personal service that Injured Iowans deserve.

For the cases that qualify, we offer a ***no cost, no obligation*** case review and evaluation of your case. We will fully explain all fees and costs to you before proceeding. Together, as a team, we will decide on the best tactics for your case.

Corey, Erik, Joanie & Nicole

WHAT IS OUR GUARANTEE TO YOU?

We will invest our time, our resources, and abilities into your case. We will even share the risk of success with you because in most cases, we will advance all the initial costs for your case. Because of this, you will be able to get your case started without paying any money out of your pocket.

This is our guarantee of commitment to you!!

Write any questions, comments, or concerns that you may have in the space below:

Page left blank intentionally.

Chapter 20

OUR CASES, VERDICTS AND RESULTS

Here are some cases that we have successfully resolved. There are others at our website at www.IowaInjured.com. Remember that each case is different. Once a case is in the hands of a jury or judge, it is out of our control. We have had cases in which we were pleasantly surprised by the verdict and others in which we were disappointed. We do not win every case and sometimes we obtain a verdict that we are not able to collect the money owed from the defendant. However, we do believe that significant trial experience and results are factors that people may use to choose one attorney over another. With these things in mind, here are some of our results which are the total amount received before the deduction of attorney fees and costs:

Personal Injury

$675,174 Verdict for Iowa State Patrol Officer Struck by an Uninsured Motorist

$675,174 verdict for an Iowa State Patrol Officer who sustained back and brain injuries in a motor vehicle accident while he was pursuing a fleeing suspect.

$312,500 Settlement for Motorcyclist

A man riding his motorcycle seriously injured his knee when a car pulled in front of him. He slid the bike on the ground to avoid the impact, but sustained a knee fracture requiring surgery and permanent knee problems.

Des Moines Police Officer Receives More than $400,000

A Des Moines police officer received more than $400,000 for injuries he sustained when he was struck by a truck while working off duty.

$4,300,000 Verdict for Car Accident Victim

A $4,300,000 verdict was handed down for a woman who suffered a broken neck causing her to be a quadriplegic when the vehicle she was a passenger in left the roadway and rolled into a ditch.

$1,363,718 Verdict for Estate of a Woman Killed by a Drunk Driver

A verdict of $1,363,718 was ordered against a drunk driver who fled the scene of a crash and was not identified until days later. The verdict included damages for the adult children of the deceased woman.

$675,000 Settlement for an ATV Driver

A man who sustained permanent brain injuries when his ATV was struck at a racetrack received a $675,000 settlement for his injuries.

Des Moines Couple Received More Than $1.4 Million

A Des Moines couple received more than $1,400,000 after they were hit head-on by another driver sustaining life threatening and permanent injuries.

$190,000 Settlement for Couple Injured on Motorcycle

A retired couple who had been married 35 years were struck from behind by a young driver not paying attention causing broken ribs and back injuries. Through mediation the couple received a $190,000 settlement.

$128,000 Verdict for a Woman with a Shoulder Injury

A Lynn County jury provided a verdict of $128,000 to a woman who injured her shoulder in a motor vehicle accident when a teenage driver pulled out in front of her. The insurance company offered her $0 prior to trial, but we obtained a verdict of $128,000 even though she had not missed any work and did not require surgery. Her husband was affected by her injuries and also received compensation for his loss of consortium.

Workers' Compensation

$310,000 Settlement for Truck Driver with Back Injury

An over the road truck driver injured his back while switching trailers which required 2 back surgeries. He sustained significant permanent restrictions and a settlement of $310,000 was reached in mediation with the driver's employer.

Judge Finds Nurse Permanently and Totally Disabled, Expected Payments of More Than $800,000

A verdict of permanent total disability was entered for a nurse providing her with weekly benefits and medical care for the rest of her life resulting expected payments of more than $800,000.

$120,000 Settlement for Worker Who Fell

A settlement of $120,000 was obtained for a man who fell at work sustaining a broken bone causing permanent medical problems.

RN Who Worked for State of Iowa Receives $400,000 Settlement After Sustaining Work Injuries

A northern Iowa Registered Nurse who worked for the state received a settlement of $400,000 and her IPERS disability pension after she was attacked by a resident causing neck and head injuries which prohibited her from returning to work for the State of Iowa.

$200,000 Settlement for Factory Worker with Neck and Shoulder Injuries

A local factory worked had sustained neck and shoulder injuries during the course of her 15 year work history. While she had physical therapy and prescription medications to treat these conditions nothing seemed to help. While the doctors did not have a surgery to fix her problems she was left with physical limitations which prevented her from returning to the factory. We were able to successfully resolve her case while preserving her health insurance benefits with her employer.

Truck Driver Receives $325,000 Settlement after 2 Failed Back Surgeries

The work injury case for a Des Moines truck driver who injured her back lifting heavy materials settled for $325,000 at mediation. She required two back surgeries and still has ongoing problems and permanent restrictions.

$125,000 Settlement for Factory Worker with an Arm Injury

A settlement of $125,000 was reached for a factory worker who was not called back to work after a work related arm injury requiring surgery resulting in permanent restrictions.

60% Disability Provided to Worker Who Sustained (2nd Injury) to Leg

A worker who had previously sustained an injury to his left leg sustained a 2nd work related injury to his right leg which resulted in him qualifying for Social Security Disability benefits. The judge determined that the worker sustained 60% industrial disability and he will be paid a total of 300 weeks of benefits totaling more than $130,000.

$120,000 Settlement After Trial and Appeal for Clerical Worker

After a trial followed by an appeal, a settlement of $120,000 was reached for a clerical worker who sustained injuries to both of her arms requiring multiple surgeries.

$150,000 Settlement For Nurse with a Back Injury

During mediation a settlement of $150,000 was reached for a nurse from Marshalltown, Iowa with a work related back injury. She required surgery and was unable to return to her same job as a nurse.

$185,000 Settlement For Injured Mechanic

After a right shoulder work injury which required 2 surgeries, a mechanic from Anamosa settled his case for $185,000 after he was required to find a new job due to permanent work restrictions.

Plumber Receives $285,000 Settlement After Fall

The workers' compensation case for a Newton plumber who fell from a ladder sustaining shoulder and back injuries was settled prior to trial for $285,000.

Jailer Receives Permanent Total Disability From 2nd Injury Fund After Being Blinded in One Eye

A Clarke County jailer is to receive a weekly workers' compensation check for the rest of her life due to an eye injury worth more than $375,000. She had previously sustained injuries to her hands which qualified her for Iowa Second Injury Fund benefits.

$415,000 Settlement for Truck Driver with Back Injury

A truck driver from Boone sustained a back injury that did not require surgery, but caused him to lose his job and the work he had always done. During mediation, a settlement of $415,000 was reached between the parties.

(**NOTICE:** PLEASE BE ADVISED THAT PAST RESULTS ACHIEVED ARE NOT A GUARANTEE OF FUTURE RESULTS. EACH CASE IS UNIQUE AND REFERENCE MUST BE MADE TO THE SPECIFIC LEGAL AND FACTUAL CIRCUMSTANCES PRESENTED. THESE RESULTS MAY NOT BE TYPICAL AND THE FACTS OF YOUR CASE ARE PROBABLY VERY DIFFERENT. THERE ARE MANY FACTORS TO CONSIDER WHEN DETERMINING THE VALUE OF YOUR CASE. THEREFORE, YOU SHOULD NOT RELY UPON THE ABOVE RESULTS IN RESOLVING YOUR CASE, BUT RATHER SHOULD CONSULT AN ATTORNEY TO DISCUSS THE SPECIFICS OF YOUR CASE AND HOW THE LAW AND FACTS APPLY TO IT.)

For a listing of more of our Cases, Verdicts and Results go to our Webpage at www.IowaInjured.com and Click on Results.

Special Report

Injured Iowans First Fee Schedule ™

A new approach of determining attorney fees in workers' compensation, car accident and other personal injury claims!

Should an attorney charge the same percentage whether they spend 2 hours or 2 years on a case?

(Of Course Not)

Walker, Billingsley & Bair
Iowa Injury Attorneys
Corey J. L. Walker, Erik D. Bair,
Joanie L. Grife & Nicole Merrill

Ankeny 2605 SW White Birch, Ste. 110
Des Moines/Urbandale 7755 Hickman Road
Marshalltown 25 North Center St.
Newton 208 N. 2nd Ave. West

Main Number- 641-792-3595

www.IowaInjured.com
Corey@IowaInjured.com

Our Injured Iowans First Fee Schedule™ in Workers' Compensation, Car Accident and Personal Injury Cases

Attorneys should charge reasonable fees based upon:

- The amount of time involved, and the results obtained
- The novelty and difficulty of the questions involved, and the skill required by the attorney to properly represent the client
- The desires and goals of the client

We have developed a revolutionary and progressive Injured Iowans First Fee Schedule™ for our work injury, car accident and other personal injury clients.

While we believe that many insurance companies will not make their best offer until we hold their feet to the fire on the eve of trial, we understand that clients have different wants and needs from an injury claim. If the attorney fees are less than the "standard fee", then the client may be able to settle his or her case sooner and still end up with the same amount of money in his or her pocket instead of waiting a year or more for a trial. While an insurance company may not be willing to pay top dollar early in the case, because the attorney is not charging the standard fee early in this case the client may choose to accept a lower amount from the insurance company. In fact, there are some cases where a percentage fee may not be the best choice. For example, in a case with a prior offer, the client may want to pay an hourly fee to the attorney which may save the client thousands of dollars in the process! This is why we developed the **Injured Iowans First Fee Schedule™** for our injury clients.

INJURED IOWANS FIRST FEE SCHEDULE™

Contingent Fee

Our **Injured Iowans First Fee Schedule™** means that the earlier your case is resolved, the lower our attorney fee percentage is. This may enable you to accept a lower settlement from the insurance company, but still come out ahead. If you tell us to, we will even advise the insurance company of our lower fee which may encourage them to make a reasonable offer to you earlier rather than later.

Note: Work Injuries/Workers' Compensation: If you are currently receiving weekly benefits, we do not take a fee on those benefits. Also, if the treating authorized physician determines that you have permanent impairment rating, and the insurance company or employer voluntarily pays that impairment rating we do not take a fee on those benefits.

Also, there is no risk to you because you do not owe us anything, unless we make a recovery for you and then it is a percentage depending on how far your case goes. For example, if your case is settled before filing a petition our percentage is lower than if we have to file a petition. If we file a petition and have a trial our percentage is lower than if we have a trial and there is an appeal.

(**NOTICE**: WE ARE NOT OBLIGATED TO APPEAL YOUR CASE AND CONTINGENCY FEES ARE PAID ON THE TOTAL RECOVERY AND ARE COMPUTED BEFORE DEDUCTING EXPENSES.)

Fewer Cases— Which Allows Us to Spend More Time For <u>You</u>

We are not your average Iowa law firm. We are "different." We have the legal know how combined with personal service and attention to details to **<u>Level the Field</u>** Between **<u>Injured Iowans</u>** and Insurance Companies.™

We don't rely on a high volume of cases. We don't claim to handle every type of law under the sun. We don't want to, and we do not need to.

Each year, we accept a limited number of serious injury, accident and work injury cases from the hundreds of people who ask us to represent them. We are not a "mill" law firm and our paralegals and assistants do not negotiate our cases with the insurance company. Fewer cases means more time for you and, we believe, better results overall.

Together, for more than 75 years we have represented personal injury, car accident, workers' compensation, and other injury clients throughout the state of Iowa. Most of the cases are referred to us by former clients and by other attorneys. If we accept your case and you are not local to us, we will come to you.

<u>Communication</u>- We take pride in having a personal relationship with our clients and communication is a key part of this. Rest assured that we will explain the legal process to you, answer all your questions, keep you informed about your case including sending you copies of letters, and usually returning your phone calls and emails within 24 hours, unless our time is being devoted to a trial.

Sometimes the best advice you can get when you are thinking about a lawsuit is that you do not have a claim that can be won. If that is true, we will tell you. We'll also tell you when we think you are better off handling a claim yourself—without an attorney. But, if your case passes our test and we accept it, you can be assured that you will receive our personal attention. We will aggressively represent you, keep you up to date on what is happening in your case, and give you our advice as to whether you should settle your case or whether we should go to trial.

We will fully explain all fees and costs to you before we start working on your case. Together, as a team, we will decide on the best tactics for your case.

Dedicated to Leveling the Field Between Injured Iowans and Insurance Companies™ by Fighting for Justice and Respect™

Fewer Cases - More Time For You

FREE Subscription Offer

Would you like to know:

- How to avoid insurance company denials;
- How to protect you and your family from financial ruin;
- Legal Insider Secrets about Iowa's laws;
- How current legal issues and cases which may affect you;
- The "inside story" about frivolous lawsuits;
- Practical advice about buying insurance from someone who does not sell insurance;
- What you must do if you are hurt at work.

These are some of the topics covered several times a year in a newsletter entitled **"The Iowa Legal Insider"** sent to your home free of charge by Walker, Billingsley & Bair. They understand and believe that most legal disputes could be avoided if people knew more about the legal system, insurance coverage and the insurance claim process.

There is absolutely no cost or obligation, and we routinely have contests to win various things including $250. There is absolutely no cost or obligation and if you subscribe and later feel like we are wasting your time, there is a phone number and an email address in every issue that you can contact to cancel. Don't worry, these are not the boring, "canned" newsletters that most firms buy and slap their name on to. We write it and we aim to provoke people to pay more attention to their legal affairs.

There is no need to destroy this book. Just photocopy this form and fill it out. Also, feel free to make extra copies to give to friends or family that may be interested. You can mail it to Walker, Billingsley & Bair 208 N. 2nd Ave. West Newton, Iowa 50208 or email the information below to Corey@IowaInjured.com. Please start my free subscription:

Name: ____

Address: ____

City:__________________________ State: __________ Zip: _______

Email: ______________________@______________________________

If you would also like to receive our email newsletter, just give us your email address. We do not share our mail/email lists with anyone!